Cambridge Elements

Elements in Shakespeare Performance
edited by
W. B. Worthen
Barnard College

PERFORMING SHAKESPEARE ON AN ENDANGERED PLANET

Katherine Steele Brokaw
University of California, Merced

Elizabeth Freestone
Shakespeare Institute, University of Birmingham

Shaftesbury Road, Cambridge CB2 8EA, United Kingdom

One Liberty Plaza, 20th Floor, New York, NY 10006, USA

477 Williamstown Road, Port Melbourne, VIC 3207, Australia

314–321, 3rd Floor, Plot 3, Splendor Forum, Jasola District Centre,
New Delhi – 110025, India

103 Penang Road, #05–06/07, Visioncrest Commercial, Singapore 238467

Cambridge University Press is part of Cambridge University Press & Assessment,
a department of the University of Cambridge.

We share the University's mission to contribute to society through the pursuit of
education, learning and research at the highest international levels of excellence.

www.cambridge.org
Information on this title: www.cambridge.org/9781009569590

DOI: 10.1017/9781009569613

© Katherine Steele Brokaw and Elizabeth Freestone 2025

This publication is in copyright. Subject to statutory exception and to the provisions
of relevant collective licensing agreements, no reproduction of any part may take place
without the written permission of Cambridge University Press & Assessment.

When citing this work, please include a reference to the DOI 10.1017/9781009569613

First published 2025

A catalogue record for this publication is available from the British Library

ISBN 978-1-009-56959-0 Paperback
ISSN 2516-0117 (online)
ISSN 2516-0109 (print)

Cambridge University Press & Assessment has no responsibility for the persistence
or accuracy of URLs for external or third-party internet websites referred to in this
publication and does not guarantee that any content on such websites is, or will
remain, accurate or appropriate.

For EU product safety concerns, contact us at Calle de José Abascal, 56, 1°, 28003
Madrid, Spain, or email eugpsr@cambridge.org

Performing Shakespeare on an Endangered Planet

Elements in Shakespeare Performance

DOI: 10.1017/9781009569613
First published online: June 2025

Katherine Steele Brokaw
University of California, Merced

Elizabeth Freestone
Shakespeare Institute, University of Birmingham

Author for correspondence: Katherine Steele Brokaw, katiebrokaw@gmail.com

ABSTRACT: Given the many environmental crises facing the planet, we need to use all tools to address them, including Shakespearean theatre. This Element explains why Shakespeare is well-positioned to be an eco-playwright, how theatre-makers can adapt his plays to matter now, and how to make more ecological the many processes of Shakespearean theatre, from set design to performing outdoors. The co-authors are both directors, and conversations between them about their recent eco-productions of *The Tempest* for the Royal Shakespeare Company and *A Midsummer Night's Dream* for Shakespeare in Yosemite (California) give clear examples of both the why and how of eco-theatrical Shakespeare.

KEYWORDS: Shakespeare, Eco-Theatre, Theatre, Shakespearean Performance, Environmental Humanities

© Katherine Steele Brokaw and Elizabeth Freestone 2025

ISBNs: 9781009569590 (PB), 9781009569613 (OC)
ISSNs: 2516-0117 (online), 2516-0109 (print)

Contents

Introduction: Discovering Shakespearean Eco-Theatre — 1

1 Why Eco-Shakespeare? — 4

2 Eco-Themes, or How to Select and Adapt Shakespearean Texts for Eco-performance — 26

3 Eco-Practices, or, How to Make Shakespeare Plays That Don't Cost the Earth — 57

Epilogue: Green Teaching — 83

Appendix A: Selected Eco-Shakespearean Companies and Organizations — 87

Appendix B: Selected Eco-Shakespearean Productions and Films — 91

Appendix C: Selected Eco-Theatre and Eco-Arts Organizations and Resources — 97

References — 98

Introduction: Discovering Shakespearean Eco-Theatre

'On such a full sea are we now afloat, / And we must take the current where it serves / Or lose our ventures' (*Julius Caesar* 4.3.253-5)

'There's a story that begins here. Or maybe it ends. It depends on us.'
– Robin Wall Kimmerer (2022)

What has Shakespeare got to do with the climate crisis? Conversely, what has the climate crisis got to do with Shakespeare? Rising seas, unstable temperatures, mass extinction, biodiversity loss, and resource shortages: these are not what first come to mind when picturing a long-dead white man with a ruff and a quill. But scratch the surface and Shakespeare's imagined worlds reveal gripping tales of geopolitical conflict and environmental catastrophe alongside vivid examples of collective responsibility and the prospect of redemption. In this Element, we make the case that Shakespeare is a dynamic and infinite cultural resource that can – and should – be reused and recycled to perform stories that will help save life on our endangered planet.

We come to this view through a shared decade of trial and error, research and practice, writing and discussion, learning and understanding. We freely admit to being fans of the plays. We also freely admit to being concerned citizens. The world is experiencing polycrises on diverse fronts: social, political, and environmental; instability is the new normal. As temperatures rise, violence and aggression correspondingly increase, while focus, productivity, and empathy decline (Rich, 2024). Amid this spiralling ecological and interpersonal disorder, we take inspiration from Donna Harraway's call to 'stay with the trouble', that is, to make the best of living and dying together on a damaged earth (2016: 77). We trust that with ingenuity and care, people can enable the kind of thinking that will build a more liveable future for ourselves and the fellow species with whom we share the planet. We come to the urgency that characterizes this Element through a belief in the power of art – and above all a belief in the power of embodied, collectively experienced storytelling – to bring communities together to make positive change.[1] Laurie Woolery, the current director of the Public Works programme in New York, says:

> I truly believe Shakespeare is a community playwright. He is the community playwright that we get to adapt into the world order that we are living in now. And the future of Shakespeare lies in continually turning to community to guide us, to lead us in interrogating what these stories have to say to the present. (2021)

Community, of course, is defined by who is in it, and we openly acknowledge that the Shakespeare community has long been guilty of being an exclusive and privileged club, gatekeeping out rather than welcoming in.[2] Throughout this Element we advocate for inclusive communities – communities of artists, whether students, amateurs or professionals; communities of audiences, in person, on tour or online; and communities of activists, volunteer, ad hoc, or organized – as the most potent force at humanity's disposal for enacting change.[3] This Element is an unrepentant call to arms, but is not intended to be dogmatic. We see ourselves as part of an existing and future eco-Shakespeare community and offer this volume as an empowering guide for theatre-makers, academics, and students working in all contexts and at all scales.

The Element is organized into three sections. The first section tackles questions of why: why storytelling, why theatre, why Shakespeare, and why Shakespeare in performance; in other words, what is it about this writer's stories and this art form that particularly speak to the climate crisis? If the opening section is the why, the following two are the how,

---

[1] Many activists write of the need for community care in a time of alienation, catastrophe, and corrupted media. See for example brown, 2017.

[2] See our next section for further discussion of how, in the words of Corredera et al., Shakespeare has been used as 'both a tool of colonial oppression and a lingua franca for those denied the right to speak overtly' (2023: xx).

[3] Sociologists have argued similarly; see for example Almeida et al., 2023.

and the Element moves into practical mode for those two sections. Section 2 is mainly focused on adapting the playscript and explores play choice, editing, production goals, and extra-textual production elements. Section 3 focuses on the material production, outdoor performances, touring, and online dissemination. A final epilogue turns to the question of teaching ecological Shakespeare.

At the ends of Sections 2 and 3 are excerpts of conversations between Katie and Elizabeth, the co-authors of this Element and directors of recent eco-productions of *A Midsummer Night's Dream* and *The Tempest* respectively. These conversations formed an extended dialogue over five days in Stratford-upon-Avon in the summer of 2024. The River Avon in Shakespeare's hometown (where Elizabeth lives and works) had just flooded after months of above-average rainfall. Meanwhile, on the other side of the world in California (where Katie lives and works), the temperature was regularly over 110 degrees Fahrenheit. As we worked on this Element and talked about our theatre-making experiences, in the evenings the skies over England glowed unseasonably red, caused by particles from North American and Canadian wildfires being transported over the Atlantic due to an unseasonably strong jet stream. Our individual experiences of working on eco-inflected Shakespeare were therefore framed by a joint experience of the climate crisis that shrank the miles which separated our productions. When we reconvened (online) in early 2025 to edit the manuscript for publication, Los Angeles was experiencing the worst wildfires in the city's history, fuelled by relentless winds and tinder-dry ground conditions. Meanwhile, the World Meteorological Organisation declared January 2025 to be the warmest on record. Drought in Sudan escalated territorial conflicts, an intense heatwave in Brazil closed schools and businesses, and the already-impoverished island of Mayotte in the Indian Ocean was devastated by Cyclone Chido. We hope the transcripts of those conversations, alongside the increased sense of urgency which shaped our rewriting process, reflect our honest endeavours to articulate how and why we think it is worth performing Shakespeare on an endangered planet.

1 Why Eco-Shakespeare?

'One touch of nature makes the whole world kin' (*Troilus and Cressida* 3.3.181)

'In order to do what the climate crisis demands of us, we have to find stories of a livable future, stories of popular power, stories that motivate people to do what it takes to make the world we need.' – Rebecca Solnit (2023)

The only place in the universe known to support life is in trouble. There's nowhere to hide, no species that is immune. Worse still, floods, drought, famine, and heat are most likely to affect humans (and non-humans) who are least responsible for the changes to our Earthly home (or, as the ancient Greeks called it, our *oikos*, from which we get our word 'ecology'). As theatre-makers and academics who teach, study, and direct Shakespeare, we have wrestled with the question: what can we do about this? And it turns out that the answer is: quite a lot.

Environmental activist, scientist, and writer Sandra Steingraber says that we are all musicians in a great human orchestra, and 'it is time now to play the Save the World Symphony. You are not required to play a solo, but you are required to figure out what instrument you hold and play it as well as you can' (1997, 289). Our instrument is Shakespearean theatre-making. In what follows, we explain:

I. Why storytelling matters to humans' ability to address environmental crises
II. Why theatre is a particularly effective kind of ecological storytelling
III. Why Shakespeare's work is inherently environmental, and finally
IV. Why Shakespearean performance is thus poised to be one way to address the crises facing our fragile ecosystems and amplify ways to meet our current environmental moment

1.1 Why Stories?

Environmental emergencies are crises of culture and narrative, not just of science and policy. An increasing amount of research indicates that compelling, persuasive storytelling is vital to ensuring cooperative environmental action (Arnold, 2018; Butfield, 2020; Moezzi et. al, 2017). Indeed, storytellers have long been at the vanguard of pushing forward environmental change. From the accessible scientific writing of Rachel Carson to the films of David Attenborough, from the poetry of William Wordsworth to Marvin Gaye's ecological anthems, from Cli-Fi (climate fiction) novels to Potawatomie botanist Robin Wall Kimmerer's books and essays, successful environmental communications have the power to not only change hearts and minds, but also to inspire local, national, and global action. International gatherings like the Conference of the Parties (COP) meetings of the UN Climate Change Conference increasingly showcase storytelling, and institutions such as the Entertainment and Culture for Climate Change Alliance (ECCA) are organizing and supporting artists and creative industries dedicated to leveraging entertainment in service of a liveable planet.

These organizations recognize that environmental communications need to be creative, not merely journalistic. In the last three decades, we have seen that communication about climate change and related, escalating threats to life on this planet have failed to lead to significant change. Genevieve Guenther, a former Renaissance literature scholar who now runs the group End Climate Silence, channels her literary training to analyse the language used by the media in its coverage of climate change (End Climate Silence, 2025). She explains that 'in Renaissance literature, there is a rhetorical principle called *energia* – energy or vividness' which means that 'if you're trying to persuade your reader, you need to give them vivid images that will capture their imaginations'. Guenther found that climate communications lacked this rhetorical strategy and were instead 'too data-driven and abstract' (qtd. in Widdicombe, 2020). While science writing and journalism are important, 'it is now widely accepted that we need creative forms of communication' (Hoydis et al., 2023: 1). Creative communication – novels, comic books, films, music, and indeed plays – can:

1) make complex scientific ideas digestible and affective
2) contextualize crises in their societies and cultures
3) activate the imagination
4) soften the edge of charged and difficult conversations

When it comes to understanding the complexities of biodiversity loss, climate change, and environmental justice, presenting the facts is not enough to inspire change. For one thing, scientific language is by nature impassive and objective, which, as Guenther explains, means that it is prone to understatement that often betrays the urgency of what is being reported (Guenther, 2024: 19). Additionally, media outlets, marketers, and politicians ignore, lie about, and politicize the realities facing our warming planet. What's more, the issues themselves are complex and our knowledge of them and the conditions themselves are rapidly changing. These things mean that gaining knowledge of environmental issues is difficult for many members of our society. But there's a deeper problem, which is the fact that, according to many psychologists, knowledge itself does not necessarily lead to action (Hoydis, 2023: 17; Pearce et al., 2017). Maxwell Boykoff explains that climate communication based primarily on conveying the facts fails at making the lived reality of climate change understandable for audiences who 'must be met where they are', and that feeling and emotion – the realm of more creative storytelling – are therefore crucial (2019, xi). Julia Hoydis, Roman Bartosch, and Jens Martin Gurr argue that neither the presentation of facts alone nor the evocation of emotion alone is enough to inspire action (2023: 10).

We believe that the combination of both facts and emotions can be more effective than either one on their own, and are also interested in Hoydis, Bartosch, and Gurr's argument that creative environmental storytelling can be most effective when it 'situates climate change within a larger cultural context' (2023: 9). For indeed, the issues facing our planet are not just scientific: humans in the global north, living in increasingly rapacious capitalistic cultures, have created these issues, and those cultures must be altered to salvage a habitable planet. Storytelling can provide a clear presentation of scientific facts, give people an emotional way to access the lived realities of those facts, *and* contextualize facts and emotions within the cultures that environmental challenges and solutions find themselves. In the words of prolific scientist and leading climate communicator Michael Mann, effective stories emphasize both *urgency*, which means presenting the situation as it is without sugarcoating, and also *agency*, which means empowering people to recognize their ability to force change, and that it's not too late to do so (Mann, 2022: 182 and passim.). Stories help us understand what has happened, what is happening, and what we can do about it.

At its best, creative storytelling doesn't merely inform, but also moves, connects, and galvanizes. When fires ravaged Los Angeles in January 2025, many pointed to Octavia Butler's prescient novel *Parable of the Sower* (1993), which writes of uncontrollable fires in LA in 2025 (Butler herself is buried in Altadena, at the epicentre of the Eaton fire). Butler's uncanny ability to predict catastrophe isn't the only reason this story mattered to the moment. Throughout her now oft-cited writings, she provides models for community care in the face of catastrophe, models that inspired a Pasadena bookstore named after her, Octavia's Bookshelf, to function as a donation centre ('Octavia Butler Imagined', 2025). Furthermore, adrienne maree brown's *Emergent Strategy* (2017) and viral activism are based on principles inspired by Butler's storytelling. The afterlives of Butler's stories have given both readers and those casually familiar with the books or brown's activism coping strategies and community practices that have been enacted in the real world.

Creative forms of communication can also help humans dream up better futures. Leading eco-critics and -novelists have often called the climate crisis a crisis of imagination: if we cannot envisage a decarbonized, cleaned up, cooperative world, we can't create it (Buell, 2005; Ghosh, 2016). Literature stimulates the imagination, and research shows that the very act of imagining can 'activate and strengthen regions of the brain involved in its real-life execution' (Bilodeau, 2020: 16). The ecological playwright Deke Weaver uses a nature metaphor to express this idea: 'Art can have tremendous long-term effects if it burrows into somebody's imagination, like a seed growing into an oak tree' (qtd. Chaudhuri and Williams, 2020: 81). Through literature, one of our best 'social technologies of imagination', we can imagine and manifest less dire futures for all Earthlings (Milkoreit, 2016: 172).

Finally, climate change is scary; conversations about it are emotionally and politically charged. Storytelling can make these conversations more human and less difficult (see Bilodeau, 2020: xv). Jessica Rivas, at the time a park ranger in Yosemite National Park, told Katie (Brokaw, co-author of this Element) after performing in Shakespeare in Yosemite's 2018 *Midsummer Night's Dream* that when you are addressing issues like climate change, and some of these very hard to accept and maybe even uncomfortable conversations – it's important that we are all included, because if we are not connected to the problem, we are also not connected to the solution ... This show addresses these [climate issues] and people are connecting to them, and it opens up conversations. I know in the conversations I've been able to have with people, I've been able to use words for this experience that aren't the same words we hear in the media, those negative narratives. (2018)

In the case of this adapted Shakespearean story, the combination of emotional, social, and naturalistic elements opened audiences up to conversations that they might otherwise find off-putting, unbelievable, or frightening.

1.2 Why Theatre?

While novels, stories, poems, journalism, and essays are important forms of climate communication, we believe that theatre is a particularly effective instrument for conveying facts, emotions, and action. There are several reasons for this:

1) Drama, both explicitly environmental plays and those that have been eco-adapted, is an effective, multi-voiced literary form that can synthesize the scientific, social, and cultural complexities of environmental crises
2) When staged, drama becomes action and is expressed and experienced by bodies in space and using the real, material world
3) The more abstract forms of representation used in the theatre allow audiences to take more imaginative leaps than they would when watching a screen
4) The process of creating and viewing theatre is collaborative, a collective rehearsal of how to navigate the challenges of a climate-inflected future

Drama has long called attention to the plight of the unjustly dispossessed (Euripides' *Trojan Women*), to the unfairness of resource shortage (Brecht's *Mother Courage*), and to the power of solidarity and activism (Tagore's

Muktadhara). With its scripting of multiple perspectives in conflict, dramatic literature is well equipped to particularize how environmental injustices and movements to resist them play out in different communities (see Angelaki, 2019: passim).

Henrik Ibsen's *An Enemy of the People* (1882) tells the story of a doctor's discovery that his town's spa waters – a major source of municipal income – are in fact being polluted and are sickening the people they purport to heal. The town leadership's refusal to close the spa and invest in clean-up – taking a major financial hit to save lives – well dramatizes tensions between economics and status (for the wealthy) and health and survival (of everyone, especially the vulnerable) that continue to be central to many environmental injustices. The play is thus considered the first deliberate eco-play. In the century and a half since it was written, explicitly environmental plays continue to be penned, many of them in the last fifteen or so years.[4] Plays like Chantal Bilodeau's *Sila* (2010), David Finnegan's *Kill Climate Deniers* (2018), Annalisa Dias's *The Invention of Seeds* (2024), and the short plays staged around the world every other year as part of Climate Change Theatre Action explicitly depict threats to the humans, animals, and plants on the frontlines of environmental crises, as well as those combatting the forces of complacency.

The practice and study of such drama has been called ecodramaturgy, a word first appearing in print when described by Theresa J. May (2010). Ecodramaturgy describes any theatrical endeavour motivated by environmental concerns and the study of it provides a 'critical framework that interrogates the implicit ecological values in any play or production' (May, 2022: 164). An ecodramaturgical production should be explicit in purpose and 'put ecological reciprocity and community at the centre of its theatrical and thematic intent' (Arons and May, 2012: 4).

Ecodramaturgy lives at the intersection of both critical and creative practice, and Catherine Love, a theatre reviewer and academic, adds that such work needs to be made and experienced on 'multiple, interconnected levels: form, content, and material conditions' if it is to be deeply felt and

---

[4] For 100 such examples, see Freestone and O'Hare, *100 Plays to Save the World*. See also May, 2021 and Kulick, 2023.

inspiring of action (2020: 228). Love suggests that such theatre should provide 'an imaginative leap, allowing us to think and feel our way through what it would mean to truly believe the facts of the climate crisis and to help develop our ability to re-imagine our way of living and being' (2021). This eco-hopeful vision of a theatre experience that offers the potential for change feels to us one worth subscribing to.

Explicitly ecodramaturgical plays are powerful ways of engaging intellectually and emotionally with environmental issues: we have both found this to be the case in the classroom, where our students read and discuss their content, from the Bhopal disaster (Rahul Varma's *Bhopal*, 2001) to the ethics of childbearing in an age of climate catastrophe (Duncan Macmillan's *Lungs*, 2011) as well as the drama's creative forms.

It is not until these plays are staged that they begin to reach their full potential and differentiate themselves from other forms of literature that only live on the page (or screen). Cognitive scientists have discovered that cognition is embodied, with learning happening via interactions of brain, body, and environment (Damasio, 2022; Macrine and Fugate, 2022). Embodied art, as Bruce McConachie writes, is therefore well placed to mobilize ecological action (2012: 98).

No form of literary art is more embodied than the theatre, which takes as its medium bodies, space, and material. The very things that are under threat in our world – the physical *contents* of eco-drama – are used to create its form. Theatre helps us think about the interactions of various bodies and materials by putting those bodies and materials in contact with each other and with the audience, and it is affected by the site in which it is performed, particularly if that site is outdoors (Fischer-Lichte, 2008; O'Malley, 2020). Being made of earthly matter both living and inert, and taking place in real space, performed theatre allows audiences a fully embodied experience.

That theatre is such a multi-sensory experience gives it a particular kind of imaginative power distinct from film.[5] We recognize the powerful reach of films – particularly popular movies; *Wall-E* (2008) and *Frozen 2* (2019), for example, both reached mass audiences with their messages

---

[5] For a cultural history of how theatre activates the imagination, see Kallenbach, 2018; for a study of this phenomenon focused on Renaissance drama, see Fanelli, 2016.

about overconsumption and Indigenous (Samí) ways of living in balance with nature. But theatre – particularly when it is staged in a way that is more suggestive than literal – leaves more room for an audience member's personal imagination to fill in the gaps. When watching plays, one's sense of the story is specifically informed by the faces and voices of the actors and the set and sound design, but the form is less representational in a way that allows spectators to personalize the story, to imagine woods, people and creatures dear to them, their own lost loves and threatened habitats. As Nicholas Ridout argues, the co-presence of actors and spectators makes theatre fundamentally ethical (Ridout, 2009: passim.).

Western theatre tends to tell linear, character-driven stories of people in conflict in particular times and places. But Amitav Ghosh suggests that environmental writers, including dramatists, need to invent new forms that better depict, convey, and communicate the crisis (2016). Theatre, or perhaps we should say performance, is equipped to experiment with such things: to use movement and myth and design and sound and multiple timeframes and interconnected locations to create new narrative forms that better speak to the peoples and issues of today. It is our contention that all kinds of theatre are needed to meet this moment: that which draws on Western forms of storytelling, that which leverages artforms and paradigms from Indigenous cultures and the Global South, new interdisciplinary genres, and work that combines some or all the aforementioned.

While no one story or play is likely to immediately turn a climate sceptic into a climate activist, stories accumulate. Guenther writes of how narratives and careful language about the climate crisis can plant seeds, which might be watered later by personal experiences or further stories real or imagined (2024). Both climate communicators and scholars of applied theatre write of how, in Helen Nicholson's words, theatre is less likely to offer an immediate and total transformation, and more likely to offer transportation, a 'travelling to another world, often fictional, which offers both new ways of seeing and different ways of looking at the familiar' (2005/14: 15). Psychologists have shown that being transported by live theatre leads to increased charitable giving and empathy as well as changes in socio-political views. One study on the matter concludes that theatre is more than mere entertainment, leading as it does to tangible increases in pro-social behaviour (Rathje et al., 2021: passim). There's an eco-Shakespearean example of this effect: in the months after the RSC *Tempest* directed by Elizabeth, the local newspaper reported an uptick in interest in litter picking that was attributed to the way that production spotlighted plastic pollution (Mingins, 2023).

Finally, the making of ecological theatre – and all theatre – is a collaborative, creative act that rehearses the very kinds of collaborative, creative acts that are needed to mitigate environmental crises. Only by working together – all humans with regard for each other and for the Earth's animals and plants – can we safeguard our planet and ourselves. Efforts to save a habitable planet reach across ideological divisions, involve improbable collaborations, and demand sacrifices and compromise. Theatre work lets us imagine stepping over psychological boundaries and ideological thresholds, rehearse for our future selves, and practice the conversation with our grandchildren about what it was like to live during the end times.

Theatre is a safe rehearsal space for both makers and audiences to role-play alternative ways of being: this is why hope and possibility are so important to communicate. All kinds of literature can depict what is possible, but in the theatre, such visions are not just fed into the singular imaginations of author and reader, but also absorbed into collective imaginations: one sees and feels their fellow audience members experiencing the same story in real time, allowing each person to sense they are part of a movement of people who care about similar things.

We humans must get in shape for what is to come: we must exercise our imagination muscles, our collaboration muscles, our empathic muscles. In the ancient origins of theatre – in Asia, in Greece, in myriad Indigenous societies – theatre was a shared space in which to work the mind, body, heart, and social imagination in service of addressing a society's problems (see also Kulick, 2023). In the intervening time, theatre has moved away from its civic function and become more internal and passive, but we need it to once again become a societal training ground.

1.3 Why Shakespeare?

What has all this embodied narrative ambition got to do with a dead white guy? We'll now go on to explore four ways in which Shakespeare's plays can be unpuzzled to speak to today's climate crisis.[6] These are:

1) His own lived experience of climate change is charted in the plays, including deforestation, the use of coal for domestic heating, and globalization
2) His lifetime was a crucible moment of human understanding of the universe, situated between Copernicus and Galileo
3) Scientists have date-stamped his time of writing to the beginnings of the Anthropocene, the geological epoch the Earth is now in
4) The content of his plays includes elemental extremities, populist power struggles, the animation of flora and fauna, and meditations on communality and the social good

Before that, though, let's do a quick rewind:

The long intellectual alliance between ecology and literature was granted its own terminology when Walter Rueckert coined the term 'ecocriticism' to describe analysing language through an environmental lens (1978, 1996). The first decades of this newly titled discipline focused on Romanticism, and re-examined the nineteenth-century poetic canon in light of industrialization and its environmental ills. Ecocriticsm then broadened to take in literary movements as diverse as Greek pastoral, the American Transcendentalists, and Sci-Fi.

The relatively newer field of Shakespearean ecocriticism emerged out of Shakespearean nature studies, quickly outgrowing straightforward interrogations of Shakespeare's abundant flora and fauna imagery to examine, for example, how weather impacts the action of the plays or correlations between Shakespeare's changing environment and our own.[7] Noting the underpinning

---

[6] For free, online podcast and blog discussions of much of the following information and more, see Borlik, 2024; *Midsummer Night's Dream*: Shakespeare and Climate Change, 2023; Daroy, 2020; and Martin, 2017.

[7] For summaries of ecocritical works of Shakespeare, see Earth Shakes Alliance (2025).

activism of many such ecocritical approaches, Gabriel Egan acknowledges the immediacy of the task at hand: 'our current environmental crisis is not merely a discourse ... but an urgent historical conjuncture that forces us to rethink the role of scholarship' (2006: 2). Ecocritical research explores issues such as ecophobia in *Othello*, *Coriolanus*, and other plays (Estok, 2011), agricultural cultivation and gendered forms of husbandry in *A Winter's Tale* (Munroe, 2016), and the concept of bastardy in the context of native and invasive species (Saenger, 2016).

These studies move between approaches as varied as place studies, geo-historical research, post-humanism, and multispecies relations, roving across disciplines with a free-wheeling energy. Despite some naysayers suggesting that early modern environmentalism is by definition anachronistic, this kind of ecocriticism, its scholars stress, is driven by the thought that 'we cannot make contact with a past unshaped by our own concerns' (Grady and Hawkes, 2007: 3). Whether any individual cares or not, environmental change dominates humans' daily experiences, on both a micro and a macro level. So how could practitioners not view Shakespeare through this prism? It would require enormous energy not to do so.

Shakespeare's texts have proven themselves to have boundless artistic longevity, relevant to a myriad of contexts. But what is it about the time in which Shakespeare was writing that particularly lets his work speak to the current ecological moment? Our proposition is that Shakespeare can be read backwards like an ecological time capsule, or forwards as a how-to guide for existing in the end times.

For one thing, he lived through the so-called Little Ice Age. This was a period of atmospheric cooling in the northern hemisphere spanning the fourteenth to eighteenth centuries, with a particularly pronounced cold snap in Shakespeare's lifetime.[8] Randall Martin draws direct lines between historical weather phenomena to illustrate the context behind the action of the plays, like the real-world failure of crop harvests that inspired the populist riots in *Coriolanus* as well as Corin's farming struggles in *As You Like It* (2015). Shakespeare's environmental experiences are embodied in

---

[8] Brian Fagan's *The Little Ice Age* (2001) is the definitive guide to this climate period.

the plays, his writer's instinct to dramatize the issues of his time means that environmental phenomena are encoded in his work. When the fairy queen Titania laments how the 'seasons alter' in *A Midsummer Night's Dream*, there is an uncanny sense of Shakespeare's lived experience of seasonal volatility speaking across the centuries (2.1.110). We are also living through a 'distemperature' (2.1.09).

Given the unsettled weather patterns around the globe then and now, certain plays are ripe for ecocritical study. There are the 'green' plays with forests, like *A Midsummer Night's Dream*, *As You Like It*, *The Merry Wives of Windsor*, and *A Winter's Tale*, and the 'blue' plays with shipwrecks, oceans, and rain like *Twelfth Night*, *Pericles*, *The Tempest*, and *King Lear*. The forest plays are seen to speak to deforestation, a practice which was ratcheting up at an alarming pace during Shakespeare's lifetime. The partial destruction of Warwickshire's Forest of Arden happened while Shakespeare was alive thanks to the Elizabethan obsession with building ships for colonizing expeditions. Several of the plays also mention enclosure, an agricultural practice that divvied up communal grazing land between individual owners. Animal husbandry intensified in this era, and Shakespeare's Midlands became the most enclosed part of England (Lipson, 1931). Then there is the concurrent and well-documented change from timber to coal to heat people's homes, a shift referenced across the plays in, for example, Mistress Quickly looking forward to 'the latter end of a sea-coal fire' (*The Merry Wives of Windsor*, 1.4.411). Such examples are specific incidences of humans altering their environment which had, and have, direct consequences both for Shakespeare's fellow planet-dwellers and ours today.

Helpfully, fictional references are backed up by a wealth of contemporaneous scientific documentation. The sixteenth century is often used as a baseline by conservation and climate organizations including the Intergovernmental Panel on Climate Change (IPCC) because this era saw hobby naturalism evolve into the emergent fields of botany, atmospherics, and zoology; several notable compendiums (see Gerard, 1597; Parkinson, 1640; Topsell, 1607) were published recording species and phenomena encountered contemporaneously. As western peoples began to spread across the world, travelogues and reportage of the lands and Indigenous peoples they encountered provide benchmarks for a pre-industrial, pre-Enlightenment, pre-globalized world. These primary records enable modern experts to draw on quantifiable source material to establish comparative datasets. It is thanks to Early Modern taxonomy that things like current extinction rates are charted with such confidence.[9]

But it's not just the biological science. Philosophically, Shakespeare helps shed light on an extraordinary moment in time. He lived his life during the fallout between Copernicus's *On the Revolutions of the Heavenly Spheres* (1543) and Galileo's condemnation (1633), when human understanding vacillated between exceptionalism and humility, supposition and knowledge, faith and fact. His astronomical peers were operating in a period of consequential debate, literally trying to figure out how the world worked, and Shakespeare was quick to embody this febrile period of discovery in his characters and stories. Hamlet's contemplation of what constitutes the 'brave o'erhanging firmament' is one such attempt to wrestle with humanity's place in the universe (2.2.1394).

The so-called New World discoveries that also characterize this time provide the most disturbing and, for us, morally imperative reason for working with Shakespeare as our climate crisis guide. Humankind is now widely acknowledged to be living in a new geological epoch. The gnat's breath of *Homo sapiens'* appearance in the timeline of the earth's long and eventful history had initially coincided with the epoch known as the Holocene but, thanks to people's unique ability to irrevocably damage their own home, humanity is now in the Anthropocene, the age of people, 'from the Greek *anthropos* meaning 'human' (Crutzen & Stoermer, 2000).[10] This title (yet to be formally approved by the International Commission on Stratigraphy) admits that the presence of carbon in ice cores, the irreversibility of plastic in sedimentary layers, and the unerasable radiation from nuclear events means humans can no longer pretend to have only had surface impact on the planet. Humans have fundamentally, geologically changed the Earth. But when exactly did this

---

[9] The IUCN's Red List and the UK Government State of Nature Report both use the 1500s as their baseline.

[10] For more on literary and humanistic approaches to the Anthropocene, and how this term refers to the story of how we got here as well as the proposed geological epoch, see Reno, 2022, 2 and passim.

shift from one geological epoch to another begin? One strong contender is Shakespeare's lifetime.

There are two conditions that must be satisfied for a new epoch to be date-marked. The first is 'evidence of long-lasting change' (tick). The second is evidence of a 'golden spike', a moment when there is a clear delineation between one geological epoch to another (Zalasiewicz et al., 2019). Some scientists think 1945 is this moment, the entrance into The Atomic Age; others look to mass industrialization in the 1800s. A third option is 1610, in a theory known as the Orbis Spike, proposed by Simon Lewis and Mark Maslin as the biocultural marker for the beginning of the Anthropocene (2015). This precise date just happens to be the year that Shakespeare wrote *The Tempest*, a play that speaks to climate concerns through the frame of European colonialism.[11]

The Orbis Spike casts the extractive behaviours of early colonial European powers as the catalytic culprit for the Anthropocene. Lewis and Maslin found their evidence in Antarctic ice cores, which show a dramatic dip in atmospheric carbon dioxide levels in 1610. They theorize this was caused by the dramatic decline in population numbers due to an estimated forty million people being exterminated during the 1500s, largely in the New World, largely because of diseases imported by European colonizers. Because many of these people were farmers, fields were no longer tended and plants and trees were able to take a greater quantity of carbon dioxide out of the atmosphere, thus resulting in a sudden downward spike in the ice records. The acknowledgement of the terrible impact of this ecological imperialism means Shakespeare's work and lifetime can be seen as coinciding with the beginning of the end times. This makes him a chronicler, a frontline cultural reporter from the moment when the Earth changed forever.

Therefore, Shakespeare is our ecological contemporary. People alive today exist in the same geological epoch and the same sixth mass extinction event as him (Kolbert, 2016). Industrialization began on his watch and has continued into ours. In her pro-presentist argument, Sharon O'Dair urges Shakespeare

---

[11] For readings of *The Tempest* in the context of early colonisation, Europeans' need for wood, and the Orbis Spike, see Nardizzi, 2013 and Linthicum, 2022.

ecocriticism to use Shakespeare's popularity to 'galvanize millions of people to act – and to do so quickly' (2011, 81). That's a way of summarizing our activist-theatre-maker stance in this Element: we learn from the historical record in the plays and apply the lessons to our present-day troubles.

Climate change, biodiversity loss, and environmental justice are complex ideas that require us to think deeply into the past and project ourselves forward into the future.[12] Equally, perspectives on the environment are diverse. There is not one solution, nor one universal global experience, nor is there collective culpability.[13] Shakespeare knows what the world is up against, socially and culturally. He dramatizes political struggles, heroes and villains, self-denial, wilful ignorance, the brave truth-telling of Kent and Paulina, the power of the people. Shakespeare's plays lend themselves to the intersectional thinking that ensures the vulnerable are not forgotten, like eco-feminist takes on *Macbeth*, interpretations of *Othello* that centre environmental racism, and eco-ableist readings of *Richard III*. These are issues which Rebecca Laroche and Jennifer Munroe describe as 'the interplay between forms of subjugation' (2017, 5).

Containing multitudes and having been appropriated for causes across political spectrums, the plays are full of precisely the sort of contradictions that will need to be navigated in the coming decades: moral clarity and consistency will be rarer than one might like. Indeed, Shakespeare himself may not have been the eco-ally we'd like him to be.[14] Because of the complexity of the work, the man, and his era, Shakespeare can be eco-appropriated in any number of ways: Shakespeare as punching bag (ooh, he's a guilty white man); Shakespeare as contemporary (ooh, he's just like us); Shakespeare as visionary (ooh, he's an eco-prophet); Shakespeare as allegory (ooh, this speaks

---

[12] For more on considerations of deep time as a tool for thinking in the Anthropocene, see Ottum, 2022.

[13] See Guenther, 2024: ix–xi on why thinking of climate change as something that the collective 'we' are doing perpetuates the fossil fuel economy.

[14] There is evidence that he advocated for the practice of enclosure, the steady privatisation of communal grazing lands and old growth forests, which deprived the majority of British people access to agricultural terrain, paving the way for the triumph of capitalism over communalism. See Fairlie, 2009; Stopes, 1918.

Performing Shakespeare on an Endangered Planet 19

to that); Shakespeare as advocate (ooh, he champions this cause). He can be any, all, and more of these things and, to be blunt, if he doesn't like it, there's nothing he can do about it.[15]

Liz Oakley Brown says that 'the question of humankind's place in and power over pre-modern and modern ecologies is a puzzle that Shakespeare's works confront' (2024: 72). We would add *perennially* confront: this out-of-copyright author with the most prominent name recognition in the history of global culture is a useful antidote to cultural amnesia. In their books, essays, and conferences, eco-critics have helped us understand Shakespeare's ecological capaciousness. Across the dizzying array of ecocritical literature, however, the most notable absent voice is the theatre-making community. When Fred Waage admits he has a 'hollow feeling that an ecocritical Shakespeare really can't affect what people feel about the environment' (2012: 219) he overlooks the places where experiential immediacy might be most readily found: rehearsal rooms and performance spaces.[16]

1.4 Why Shakespeare Theatre?

Lighting the Way, a collection of Climate Change Theatre Action (CCTA) plays from 2019, documents how many productions of their new plays about the climate crisis had trouble with ticket sales. CCTA are considering changing their name to make it more appealing to people who don't want to see a 'gloomy' climate play. They also found that 'the majority, if not all, of the audience was likely to be sympathetic to the cause of climate change action' (Bilodeau, 2020: 46).

If the main barrier to climate-inflected theatre is that not many people want to see it, and that those few who do are members of the proverbially pre-converted choir, what's to be done?

---

[15] Though as Corredera et al suggest, 'one imagines that Shakespeare, who routinely appropriated and exploited his own sources, would surely not mind', 2023, xix.

[16] In 2015, ecocritic Randall Martin wrote that 'Shakespeare's greatest possibility for becoming our eco-contemporary, however, arguably lies not in academic discourse but in performance', and lamented how few productions had at that point experimented with Shakespeare as an eco-contemporary (167).

Enter Shakespeare.

Our gambit is that 'who wants to see some Shakespeare?' is more likely to induce an affirmative answer than 'who wants to see a climate change play?' That might be, for many people, a choice between the lesser of two evils, but in the face of the rising seas, we'll take the good where we can. Performed Shakespeare has several advantages as a form of environmental communication:

1) The name recognition factor, ubiquity, and canonicity of Shakespeare can be deployed to maximize impact
2) Shakespeare's out-of-copyright works can be infinitely adapted in ways that speak to both local and global contemporary concerns
3) Shakespeare has a 'Trojan Horse' capacity that invites larger audiences to see his plays than might see a new, environment-specific play, and can evade censorship
4) Shakespeare is often performed outdoors, allowing plays to draw attention to the natural world in real time

The bare truth is that most people around the world, of whatever nationality or background, have heard of Shakespeare. Most adults can name some play titles, and many even have a sense of a few plots. People tend to know, for example, that *Romeo and Juliet* is, to misquote Lady Gaga, some kind of sad romance. There's a general sense that *A Midsummer Night's Dream* has fairy comedic vibes. There is a long global history of student, amateur, community and professional Shakespearean theatre-making, as well as famous actors taking on his iconic roles on stage and on film. Your local dentist might have played Juliet, and so has Claire Danes. This hypercanonicity can be leveraged.[17] Instead of shying away from this ubiquity, it can be carefully used to tell urgent new stories about the planet. As Alys Daroy and

---

[17] The term 'hypercanonicity' is attributed to Sanskrit scholar Sheldon Pollock (2015). We reframe it here to speak to the Shakespeare canon. Martin and O'Malley write about leveraging Shakespeare's canonicity for eco-performance, 2018, 386.

Paul Prescott write, 'this is not a question of ancestor worship, but species survival' (2025: 2).

Harnessing Shakespeare's social capital also means wrestling with the fact that Shakespeare has long been weaponized. People's initial encounter with his works is often deeply problematic. The language is a barrier, making people feel excluded, denied access due to the difficulty of the dense diction and twisted syntax (more on this in Section 2). The British used him to force the English language and its poetry upon its millions of subject-inhabitants in its global empire, and he continues to be used as a tool of cultural oppression and suppression in some regimes today. This imperial legacy draws on the traditional, hierarchical, Christian worldview that Shakespeare was writing from and wields it to exert social dominance and project an image of cultural superiority. His work contains some deeply offensive material including racist, misogynist, and ableist language and themes, as well as myriad examples of 'othering'. To see the canon as a simplistic vehicle for social justice, and to rely solely on a general, liberal understanding of the texts is to whitewash this history and deny these aspects of Shakespeare's legacy. Using Shakespeare justly requires clear eyes about the ways he has been used unjustly (Espinosa, 2021; Ruiter, 2021; Thurman and Young, 2023).[18] We do not advocate for exonerating Shakespeare or his work from this legacy, but instead acknowledge it, teach it to our students, and handle it carefully and intentionally in our production processes.

We take inspiration from the way Shakespeare has been used in a kind of reverse appropriation: artists have re-engineered his work to speak to democracy and human rights and to take umbrage with the dominant social group.[19]

---

[18] Several networks of scholars have been grappling with the racism of Shakespeare's plays as well as of Shakespeare studies as an academic field. See the Early Modern Scholars of Colour Network (About EMSOC, 2025) and Arizona State University's RaceB4Race (RaceB4Race, 2025)

[19] Echoing several scholars who argue a similar point, Vanessa Corredera, Monique Pittman, and Geoffrey Way write that while Shakespeare's works have been appropriated by dominant groups to subjugate and oppress, they also have a long history of being appropriated by subordinate groups as part of

Examples include the adaptive work of Chicanx playwrights (see Borderlands Shakespeare Collectiva, 2024), the Indigenous American company Amerinda, and the way Shakespeare was used in the context of Delhi's Shaheen Bagh protests in 2019 or the Umbrella Democracy protests in Hong Kong in 2014. A more specific recent example: Argentine director Monica Maffia's production of *Cymbeline* framed Shakespeare's story through a contemporary Argentine perspective by drawing on an Indigenous origin story which replaced Shakespeare's Christian and Roman gods with those from the Tehuelchen mythological pantheon. By reclaiming divine authority, this adaptation created a counter-narrative that translated the exploitative European behaviours in *Cymbeline* into an empowering anti-colonial gesture. These examples all utilize Shakespeare's broad appeal and universal name recognition to speak directly to abuses of power, tyranny and oppression.

There is one simple reason why it is possible to both wrestle with and reappropriate Shakespeare in this way: he is out of copyright (in fact, his work predates the idea of copyright, so he has never been *in* copyright). The artistic freedom that comes with this, and the fact that there are no royalties to be paid for performing his plays, goes hand in hand with the ubiquity of his work. Shakespeare is an endlessly renewable cultural resource. Rewrite *Romeo and Juliet* and you haven't damaged the one Shakespeare wrote. There are of course many other writers who are similarly out of copyright, from Indigenous tellers of folktales to ancient Greek dramatists to nineteenth century icons like Ibsen and Chekhov. There are also writers contemporaneous to Shakespeare who wrote plays that might be easily eco-appropriated, like Christopher Marlow's *Doctor Faustus* and John Heywood's *The Play of The Weather*, amongst others. But none of these has the global name recognition factor of Mr. W.S.

Not only can Shakespeare's plays legally be adapted in myriad ways, but also they lend themselves to this practice. To borrow Emma Smith's useful phrase, his plays are full of 'gapiness' (2019: passim). He never seems to quite come down on one side or the other. Audiences find themselves cheering on both king and rioting populace, moved by Bottom's terrible

a 'positive process' examining power structures and exploiting Shakespeare's cultural capital (2023: xix–xx).

acting, or laughing at the mass murderer *Richard III*. Right and wrong isn't binary and the mess of humanity in all its charms and contradictions is on display. This interpretive promiscuity offers multiple opportunities for theatre-makers to create all sorts of meanings out of these plays that are relevant to the twenty-first century.

Shakespearean adaptations can be heavily localized, allowing us to see ourselves as part of both our own ecosystem and the worldwide eco-network, and, conversely, to think about how global decisions affect local realities. Unlike a new eco-play, for example, his words can be adapted, becoming bespoke for the community by and for which they are performed; they can meet people where they are and speak to their particular climate realities. The plays aren't universal, but they are malleable; to use Emily Greenwood's helpful neologism, they are 'omni-local' (2016: 43–44).

Shakespearean drama can do many things at once. Thinking back to the climate science history encoded in the plays, they can be factual; but thinking of theatre's potent ability to make change, they can be affective. Eco-Shakespearean productions can inform but shouldn't only inform. They can rail at past injustices, grieve current pains, and offer hope. They offer opportunities for the voiceless more-than-human world to be heard. They create a place in which a sense of past, present, and future come together to invite people into the conversation (for a free comic book version of the aforementioned thoughts, see Brokaw and Curington, 2024).

The Shakespearean collision of past and present, Lynne Bruckner writes, 'is Shakespeare in the ecotone – letting the archival and presentist collide, even compete, to achieve something that matters' (2011: 245). Theatre-makers have long been best poised to 'achieve something that matters' in this way. For modern-day theatre-makers, Shakespeare has never been relegated to the deep past; his writer credit is listed in the programme alongside the lighting designer and actors. Diana Henderson calls this practice a way to 'collaborate with a dead man' (2006: 8). His is a live presence in real-time, real-world dialogue with the fellow creative voices in the rehearsal room, where the required leaps of imagination are easy to make. If global warming is a 'literary problem', as Bill McKibben claimed long ago (1989: 158), the theatre-making environment might be the best place in which to marry the time for analysis with the imperative for action.

Simple as this solution sounds, the notion raises questions. What is an ecodramaturgical production? One in which environmental themes are amplified through textual, production, or performance choices? A production which has been created using low-carbon production techniques? Is it simply a production that takes place outside, that is, *in* the environment? We suggest all and any of these can be ecodramaturgical if they want to be. Why argue about what to call the fire when there is a *fire*? Taking in past, present, and future, theatre-makers can construct fictional worlds in ecologically responsible ways while amplifying environmental narratives both inherent in, and transposed onto, the text.

This eco-adapted Shakespeare can find an audience. Shakespeare's plays have much to teach us about our environmental moment, but this is not immediately obvious to most. This is a theatrical advantage. Not everyone wants to hear about the climate emergency, either through denial, exhaustion, anxiety or censorship. As we were finishing revisions of this Element in February 2025, the US federal government had begun issuing orders to universities and arts organizations receiving federal grants that they needed to stop talking about environmental justice and climate change or face defunding or even investigation. In the contexts of both understandable climate fatigue and the malicious suppression of environmental truths, Shakespeare can be a useful Trojan horse. The cover granted by this politically neutral-seeming, canonical author allows theatre-makers to dodge censorship and reach people who wouldn't otherwise listen, or didn't know they were able to hear. Many companies have realized that Shakespeare is one of the theatre-making community's best hopes for making a meaningful contribution to saving a habitable planet, and their work is highlighted in this Element and documented in appendices A and B (see also Daroy and Prescott, 2025 and Martin and O'Malley, 2018).

Finally, these inherently ecological plays are often performed outdoors (see Figure 1).[20] There is a long global tradition of outdoor Shakespeare: audiences gathering under the stars, as Shakespeare's audience would have done at the open-roofed Globe Theatre in London, to experience tales of

---

[20] For an explanation of the inherent theatricality of wilderness, see Sweeting and Chrochunis, 2001.

Performing Shakespeare on an Endangered Planet

Figure 1 Shakespeare in Yosemite's outdoor setting in Curry Village, Yosemite National Park. Photo credit: Shawn Overton

love and wonder, power and magic. Because most of the plays were originally staged in the open air and with little in terms of set, they can *still* be staged in the open air, with little in terms of set. These royalty-free plays are not only adaptable, but portable.

Outdoor-situated Shakespeare provides many opportunities to draw attention to local ecological conditions, be that the difference between the weather as presented in a play and the weather as experienced by the audience (O'Malley, 2020), a production location's flora and fauna (Macfaul, 2015), or the visible impacts of industry and environmental policy (Borlik, 2024). Shakespeare productions happen around the world, on beaches or in city parks, upon grass or tarmac, for passers-by or paying public; all of these locations can be leveraged to relate the play's world to the audience's immediate environment.

As we wrote previously, we recognize that a play's impact on audience members is hard to measure, and that it is rare that a work of art will, upon one's first encounter with it, completely change someone's mind. But works of art – including works of adapted Shakespeare – can provide information, provoke new feelings, and inspire more prosocial behaviour. These might be called micro-progressions.[21] And they add up.

The great Afrofuturist writer Octavia Butler was once asked, 'well, what's the answer?' 'There isn't one,' she replied. 'No answer? You mean we're just doomed?' She smiled. 'There's no single answer that will solve all our future problems. There are thousands of answers, at least. And you can be one of them if you choose to be.' All Shakespearean theatre-makers can be one of the answers. This section has shown why, and the next two sections will show how.

2 Eco-Themes, or How to Select and Adapt Shakespearean Texts for Eco-performance

'Nature should bring forth / Of its own kind all foison, all abundance' (*The Tempest* 2.1.179–80)

'If we were able to unshackle our imaginations in this moment, I think our compatibility with the Earth would become possible' – adrienne maree brown (2023: 151).

This section focuses on adapting Shakespearean plays into ecological dramas. When it comes to selecting and adapting a Shakespeare play so that it can address environmental issues, we believe that productions should be

---

[21] This term, first used in sport psychology to describe incremental progress (Wylleman et al., 2013), is now often applied to education (Childress et al., 2020), as well as in relation to conscious and unconscious biases. Microprogressions are '[s]mall, regular, and common acts or experiences that serve to challenge and/or dismantle bias, stereotypes, discrimination, as well as oppression.' (Strunk et al., 2017: 211).

hopeful, goal-oriented, accessible, and energizing.[22] Preparing a Shakespearean playscript for ecological adaptation thus involves four processes:

I. Selecting a play that can end with hope, however fragile, rather than despair
II. Setting intellectual, emotional, and social goals for a production, and building a cast and team who can best reach these goals
III. Adapting Shakespeare's text(s) by cutting, lightly amending, and even importing lines from other plays
IV. Enlivening shows with extra-Shakespearean elements like new writing and music

After describing each of these, this section concludes with a discussion between us, Elizabeth and Katie, about why we were drawn to *The Tempest* and *Midsummer Night's Dream,* respectively, for our productions for the Royal Shakespeare Company (2023) and Shakespeare in Yosemite (2024); our goals for these productions; and how we used the text and extra-textual elements to adapt our shows.

2.1 Play Selection: A Case for Comedy and Tragicomedy

The climate crisis is more terrifying than any horror film. The loss of lives – human and non-human – from heat, pollution, fire, and flood is tragic. The fight against the forces of greed and indifference that cause these tragedies is epic. And Shakespeare gives us plays with barren heaths, monstrous storms, gruesome deaths, rapacious behaviour, and the consequences of taking 'too little care of these things' (*King Lear* 3.4.38). Yes, tragedies can be steered ecologically: the National Theatre's 2018 *Macbeth*, LaTrobe University's 2017 *King Lear*, and Montana InSite Theatre's 2019 *Timon of Anaconda* were all powerful pieces of ecological theatre (see Appendix B). However, we suggest that comedy and tragicomedy are best suited to making eco-theatre because:

1) Feelings of despair, which genres like tragedy and horror provoke, do not necessarily motivate action

---

[22] For another perspective on eco-directing canonical plays including Shakespeare, see Cless, 2012.

2) Shakespearean comedies and tragicomedies often evoke what Northrop Frye famously called 'the green world' (1957), and lend themselves to the idea of earthly stewardship
3) Comedies and tragicomedies often feature imagination-stretching moments of the fantastic that can expand people's sense of possibility
4) Comedies and tragicomedies feature the social actions needed to build a more just world, like forgiveness, love, and community repair

Psychological research has shown that despair, a feeling one may be left with after a brutal experience of tragedy, can inhibit action and empathy (Hoydis, 2023: 17). And in terms of their imaginative capacity, tragedies are not particularly helpful; in Chantal Bilodeau's words, 'if we only imagine the worst, the worst is what we're going to create' (2020: 18). We know that productions can do more than make us depressed, fearful, or resigned to a grim fate. Rebecca Solnit, in calling for new and hopeful climate stories, writes that 'apocalyptic thinking is due to another narrative failure: the inability to imagine a world different than the one we currently inhabit' (2023). It is not that eco-productions of Shakespeare should avoid provoking feelings of grief and fear in audiences, and in fact both of us have found it crucial to stage moments of eco-grief in our productions, to invite our audiences to join our actors in mourning what has been lost. That grief makes the play's hard-won hope both more realistic and more emotionally powerful.

Additionally, many of Shakespeare's comedies and tragicomedies borrow tropes and ideas from one of the oldest and most persistent literary subgenres: the pastoral. From the garden of Eden to medieval visions of paradise (a word that literally means enclosed park) to the forest of Arden, stories of retreat into wilderness that leave people better reconciled to each other and to their natural world are naturally ecological. The pastoral mode is not unproblematic: these stories often dangerously erase the presence and labour of Indigenous peoples, and they can reinforce imagined divisions of civilization from uninhabited wilderness that distract people from the reality that we are all dependent upon complex ecosystems for survival (John Muir's accounts of Yosemite are a classic example of both these pastoral pitfalls). Terry Gifford thus proposes that contemporary artists might aim for a 'post-pastoral' that suggests 'a collapse of the human/nature divide', a kind of literary experience that recognizes the interconnectedness of all environments, from urban to rural to protected wilderness (2014: 26). Shakespeare's comedies and tragicomedies are ripe for being adapted into post-pastoral stories. We might also think about how Shakespearean performance can be pastoral in both senses of the word, by evoking both the so-called green world and the need to care for it.

Comedies and tragicomedies are also laden with what Timothy Clark describes as 'modes of the fantastic' that can break down distinctions between character and environment, showing humans' connectedness to the world around them (2014: 81). Tales of wonder have a long tradition, from Indigenous creation myths to medieval tales of Celtic Otherworlds and Arthurian stories like *Sir Gawain and the Green Knight*, all of which often overlay pastoral conventions with the fantastic (Siewers, 2014: 31). Shakespeare's comedies and tragicomedies are full of fantastical moments – descending gods, flying fairies, the entrance into a forest – that allow theatre-makers to stage what Deke Weaver calls 'plain old wonder' that provoke 'awe at the mystery and enormity of all that we are about to lose' (qtd. Chaudhuri and Williams, 2020: 80, 81). In reminding us of the precious splendour of things greater than ourselves, these feelings of awe can also inspire resolve to save what's threatened. For indeed, psychologists have shown that feelings of awe – induced most consistently by vast landscapes and complex works of art – make people feel humbler, kinder, and more cooperative (Allen, 2018).

The emotional arc of comedies and tragicomedies might also prompt audiences to leave the theatre feeling humbler, kinder, and more cooperative. As a society, it is important that we move from narratives of catastrophe and dystopic aftermaths and instead imagine collaborative solutions, something that is seen in numerous Afrofuturist and Indigenous stories and novels. Adapted Shakespearean comedies can be solution narratives, too. These stories show humans working together to overcome grief, fear, and strife. They stage intergenerational forgiveness and community repair, and, as a final image, give audiences the heartening sight of a massive number of very much alive people on stage.

A survey of audiences who attended Climate Change Theatre Action events in 2019 revealed that the most popular elements of these short plays involved humour, community, or hope (Bilodeau, 2020: 45); year after year, Shakespeare in Yosemite's audience surveys say much the same. Many spectators write about how being in community while experiencing a story that ends with hope gives them a renewed and motivating sense of solidarity and possibility.

The hope that we speak of when we talk about the endings of eco-Shakespearean plays is not naive optimism. It is closer to what Rebecca Solnit, in her book of the same title, calls 'Hope in the Dark', a hope 'with an imagination adequate to the possibilities and the strangeness and the dangers on this earth at this moment' (2004, 5). When we speak of humour, we do not suggest provoking laughter that is facile or gratuitous. Writing about the eco-possibilities of the medieval play of Noah's flood put on by the citizens of Wakefield, England, Brian Kulick explains that 'laughter both draws us in and opens us up. We collectively let down our guard when we laugh. At that point, the author can now speak of more serious matters' (2023: 85). In our own work and conversations with audiences, we have found that both humour and music function in the heart-opening, community-building way Kulick describes, and this observation is borne out by sociological research (Chattoo et al., 2020).

2.2 Setting Intellectual, Emotional, and Social Goals for a Production and Building a Team

Once a play is chosen, the leadership team sets their goals for the production, which will inform choices related to adapting the script, casting, rehearsing, designing, and marketing. The previous section proposed that ecological theatre can:

1) Inform audiences of environmental truths (the science), as well as the biological and political challenges that both complicate and enable environmental solutions
2) Prompt people to have emotional, empathetic experiences related to ecological crises and their impact on the human and more-than-human world
3) Contextualize environmental crises in particular communities to provoke senses of solidarity and determination, inspiring action and discouraging complacency

In addition, it is crucial that a production's leadership

4) Build an inclusive on- and off-stage team that is representative of the community's demographic and social diversity

Ideally, when adapting Shakespeare ecologically, a director has clear goals for categories 1–3: they have thought through what they want audiences to learn, some of the things they hope they feel (emotional responses will of course vary among spectators), and how they want them to link this learning and emotion to their own community in a way that inspires resolve and action.

When casting the show and recruiting the behind-the-scenes designers and crew, it is important to practice what Alys Daroy and Paul Prescott call 'ecological casting', that is, building casts and teams that reflect the production's home or *oikos* (2025: 140). The people working on a show should bring myriad lived experiences to the process, and audiences should see a reflection of their world's diversity on stage. It is not just that audience members are likely to feel more included and motivated if they see themselves on stage, but also that women and people of colour are on the frontlines of ecological calamity and the fight for environmental justice, and – deviating from casting in Shakespeare's day – should be well represented in a production's decision-making process and cast.

Throughout the production process, the team can think through how their goals interact with each other: how ecological information interacts with the kind of emotional experience some scenes might provoke, and how the knowledge gained and feelings provoked are rooted in a particular time and place that audiences will care about, be that the time and place of production (like California in 2024, for Shakespeare in Yosemite's *Dream*, see Figure 2) or another time and place needing the world's attention (like island nations on the frontlines of the climate crisis in the RSC's 2023 *Tempest*). Every audience member walking out of a production might not be able to articulate what they learned from it, how they felt about what they saw, or their newfound resolve in any consistent way, and nor should they. A diversity of audience responses indicates that a show is not mere propaganda, and that spectators represent a variety of backgrounds and experiences. Nonetheless, having

Figure 2 Cast and crew of A *Midsummer Yosemite's Dream*, Yosemite National Park, 2024. Photo credit: William Serg George

intellectual, emotional, and social aims for a production can productively focus a team on how best to convey environmental crises and solutions.

2.3 Adapting with Shakespeare's Language

Many of Shakespeare's plays are full of ecological language: John of Gaunt's lament for the leased out land, Jaques' concern for the deer, the famine in Tarsus in *Pericles*. These passages are productive for ecocritical readings by scholars and students who can slow down to parse them, understand them, and research their historical contexts. But when performed in early modern English surrounded by the plays' many other words, the ecological language of Shakespeare is limited in its power to inspire ecological thinking and action (see Minton, 2021). It is for this

Performing Shakespeare on an Endangered Planet 33

reason that we believe these texts need some adaptation, and have found it useful to:

1) Cut plays so that what matters most to the plot and the production's aims remains, and confusing and offensive material is addressed, reframed, or excised
2) Bring a play's ecological language forward and work with actors to reinterpret passages so that they speak to our contemporary environmental and social moment
3) Import language from other Shakespearean plays and early modern texts
4) Adapt or translate language to be accessible and comprehensible to audiences

Don't panic. Shakespeare will be fine, no matter what we do to his plays. They cannot be exhausted for future generations, but they can be infinitely adapted to portray the challenges faced by our many fragile *oikoi* (homes).

These plays are not without problems, not without language that is misogynist, racist, heteronormative, and even anti-ecological. Indigenous American theatre-maker Madeline Sayet reminds us that 'within Shakespeare's plays, we find both rationality and understanding of the natural world's connectedness to our behaviour and colonial ideas that move us toward a destructive, extractive world'. She reminds us that theatre-makers get to choose what to do with these plays and 'we must return our thinking to the circle, instead of being extractive with Shakespeare' (2021). Returning our thinking to the circle means highlighting when Shakespeare's plays engage with the more-than-human world: when Titania's enchantment with Bottom 'evokes the most benign possibilities for humanity's engagement with nature' (Watson, 2011: 45), when *Hamlet* 'explores the thin line that separates the human from its imagined primate original' (Dionne, 2020: 316), or when the plays are simply what Alys Daroy calls 'biophilic' and celebrate the wonder of the natural world (2022). We also want to theatrically emphasize moments of cooperation and forgiveness that model the kinds of behaviour needed to mitigate and make more equitable the crises facing our communities. Because such moments can be found across genres, we both find ourselves importing lines from other plays: bits of *Troilus and Cressida*, *Richard II*, *Hamlet*, and *The Tempest* found their way into the 2018 and 2024 productions of *Dream* for Shakespeare in Yosemite, and Elizabeth's 2023 *Tempest* for the RSC borrowed from the sonnets and *Dream* (see Figure 3).

Cutting away what is not relevant to a production's ecological goals and primary storytelling can allow Shakespeare's language, when paired with clearly focused acting, to make new ecological meanings (see also Brokaw and Prescott, 2022). For most spectators who see a Shakespearean play performed in English (and here translated, non-Anglophone Shakespeare has an advantage!), most of what they are hearing is somewhere between mildly baffling to utterly incomprehensible. That is no one's fault: Shakespeare's plays are well over 400 years old, and next to no one living in the twenty-first century, be they a native English speaker or not, can fully comprehend them when listening to them, unglossed and at speed. However, when it comes to effective eco-theatre, it is crucial that audiences understand what they are hearing.

Figure 3 Alex Kingston as Prospero, *The Tempest*, Royal Shakespeare Theatre, 2023. Photo credit: Ikin Yum

With most spectators, theatre-makers don't win points for being faithful to Shakespeare's language, but they lose points for being incomprehensible, for making audiences feel stupid and excluded. We therefore want to inspire eco-theatre-makers (and all theatre-makers) to adapt and translate Shakespeare's language when it helps audiences feel included in the story, and therefore included in environmental crises and solutions. That might mean changing 'thou dost' to 'you do', 'exempt from public haunt' to 'outside the busy town', or indigenizing references to place, flora, and fauna to refer to the community and ecosystem in which a play is being performed. Shakespeare is super dead: he won't care.

2.4 Adapting beyond Shakespeare's Language

Shakespearean texts give us a lot of effective raw material for creating eco-theatre: descriptive ecological language, stories of power struggle and cooperation, multilocational plotlines. But because these plays are out of copyright, theatre-makers need not limit themselves to working only with Shakespeare's language (including translated and adapted language). When it suits their intellectual, emotional, and social goals, theatre-makers should feel free to:

1) Collaborate with non-Shakespeareans – activists, frontline community members, scientists – to best adapt the script
2) Rewrite the text to make it more clearly evoke particular ecosystems, communities, and environmental crises and solutions
3) Write new lines that convey environmental storylines and information
4) Use music and dance to enhance feelings of grief, hope, and solidarity

The goal here is to help preserve life on Earth, not resuscitate Shakespeare, and theatre-makers should do whatever is needed to create the most effective eco-theatrical experience. In rewriting old stories to address the various crises of our world, we are doing what Shakespeare did for early modern England.

While there is much to be gained from reading ecocritical scholarship and turning to Shakespeare's texts for inspiration, we have found that it is also important to collaborate with non-Shakespeareans whose expertise and life experiences can inform our productions. Katie's team includes scientists and park rangers whose work on red-legged frogs, forest fires, and giant sequoias is central to Shakespeare in Yosemite's productions; Elizabeth consulted with the Recycled Orchestra of Cateura in Paraguay, the UK Woodland Trust, and other global and local environmental organizations. Working with experts and people with firsthand experience of environmental catastrophe allows us to adapt and perform texts that are more truthfully rooted in particular communities near and far, evoking the challenges of our living world rather than Shakespeare's long lost past. An audience member needs to mourn more than the deforestation of Shakespeare's forest of Arden, feel wonder beyond the fairy Peaseblossom: ideally, they think of threats to their own most beloved landscapes, awe at creatures in their backyard.

Adaptation of language can do some of this collapsing of real and imaginative worlds. From a stage surrounded by trees, Shakespeare in Yosemite's Juliet gazed at what she was describing when she exclaimed 'that which we call a ponderosa pine by any other name would smell as sweet!' (see Figure 4). But that production, being about the reintroduction of the near-extinct red-legged frogs to the Sierra ecosystem and not about teen suicide, was also full of language that Katie and her park ranger collaborators invented wholesale. Some of it was borrowed from Shakespeare ('when it comes to biodiversity loss, all are punished'). Some of it was not. The production's goals guided all textual choices: the team was more loyal to the living creatures of 2023 than to the memory of Shakespeare.

In South Africa, the Joburg Theatre Youth Development Programme's production of *Macbeth* (2021) employed adaptive ecodramaturgy to decolonize the play. The numerous bird species that Shakespeare names, often for their familiar symbolic associations in Europe, were found to resist relatable decoding in the South African context. Director Sarah Roberts describes how the ensemble found that Banquo's comment on the curious phenomenon of a nesting martlet as he approaches Glamis castle 'lacked purchase for a local audience' and only seemed to 'stress distances between the play and a South African audience' (2022: 6). The lines were cut, recoded, and replaced by avian references that allowed the multi-lingual company – who performed the play in English, Zulu, Xhosa and Sesotho as well as other languages – to 'render the text without alienating listeners or undercutting the value of local, experiential knowledge' (ibid.: 6–7).

Performing Shakespeare on an Endangered Planet 37

Figure 4 Madelyn Lara as Juliet, *Romeo and Juliet in Yosemite*, Yosemite National Park, 2023. Photo credit: Grace Garnica

While adapted and newly scripted words can go a long way towards moving an audience towards theatre-makers' intellectual, emotional, and social aims, use of music and dance can further them even more. In a book on what he calls 'ecomusicology', Mark Pedelty quotes several people describing how specific songs spurred them to environmental action and informed them of things they didn't know about; 'clearly, musical knowledge can translate into action' (2012, 61). Pedelty ultimately concludes that music is more ecologically inspiring when yoked to other artforms: 'Ecomusicology needs to look toward music's intertextual connections. Music becomes even more meaningful when joined with other arts, media, and activities' (204).

We have found through both practice and study that music joined with Shakespearean theatre can be a catalysing conveyer of ecological messaging, as can other extra-Shakespearean elements.

We have argued that these plays are inherently ecological, and that they could use some adaptation to make them into more effective pieces of ecotheatre. Wholesale requisition of an original work that is then appropriated for entirely different purposes indicates a deliberate schism between source material and copy (think of *King Lear* and *Succession*). Adaptation, however, as understood by literary and performance studies, describes how imaginative re-contextualization roots its endeavours in a presupposed relationship to an original source (see Leitch, 2017). Just as an organism cannot outgrow its original DNA, an adapted Shakespeare play does not deny its parent but intentionally draws attention to any interventions made in an attempt to sharpen the audience's response to the source material as well as its new iteration (Carroll, 2009). Eco-adaptation, therefore, seeks to both amplify the plays' manifold examples of existing environmental content and intensify their eco-theatrical potential through addition and/or re-contextualization. Original work may be effective at communicating a specific example, but adaptation invites the audience to witness both the source and the intercession, the extant alongside the potential alternative. Shakespeare understood this well and was himself an expert adapter, drawing on multiple extant sources such as classical mythology, English folk tales, and historical chronicles to craft his narratives, many of them familiar to his audience.[23] We suggest that Shakespeare's own expertise in adapting source material to speak to his contemporaneous concerns sets an empowering example for the modern theatre-maker to follow.

Adapting *Dream* and *the Tempest*: A Conversation

Having seen each other's shows, in summer 2024 we sat on the banks of the Avon in Shakespeare's hometown and interviewed each other about them. For context, here is some basic information about each show:

---

[23] For more on academic debates about Shakespearean adaptation, see Henderson and O'Neill, 2022 and Kidnie, 2009. For a how-to guide for writing adaptations, see Goldfinger and Horsley, 2023.

Performing Shakespeare on an Endangered Planet 39

Figure 5 Jessica Rhodes as Miranda and Alex Kingston as Prospero in *The Tempest*. Royal Shakespeare Theatre, 2023. Photo Credit: Ikin Yum

The Tempest, directed by Elizabeth, played at the RSC's Royal Shakespeare Theatre from January to March 2023.[24] It starred Alex Kingston as a female Prospero, who with her daughter had to navigate the perils of a polluted, climate-ravaged island (see Figure 5).

A Midsummer Yosemite's Dream, directed by Katie, played on the University of California Merced campus and in the amphitheatre of Yosemite National Park's Curry Village in April 2024.[25] It took as its starting point the archival discovery that director Max Reinhardt declined an invitation to stage Dream in front of Yosemite falls in 1934. Ninety years

---

[24] For more on this production, see Lawson 2023, Green 2023, Bradley 2024, and *The Tempest*, 2024, website.

[25] For more on this production, see Freestone 2025, Werth 2024, and *A Midsummer Yosemite's Dream*, 2024, website; the full production can be viewed on YouTube on the @yosemiteshakes channel.

later, this musical adaptation imagines a collision of 1930s fairies with 2024 Ranger Mechanicals and lover-tourists.

Elizabeth: Why do *A Midsummer Night's Dream*?

Katie: Fundamentally both *Dream* and *As You Like It* are about people going into the woods and coming out better people, and that's what the National Park Service wants to happen when one visits a protected wilderness. There's something about that experience that puts you in touch with things that are bigger than yourself. And more than any other play, *Dream* calls attention to the nonhuman world. It has fairies that are named after plants and animals, and Titania's speech about the changing seasons. And there's name recognition: of all the comedies, it's the most popular. It is also a celebration of amateur drama, which is what we do.

What draws you to *The Tempest* as an eco-play in terms of both its early modern contexts and how it speaks to present-day ecological crises we face?

Elizabeth: It starts with this famous stage direction about the tempestuous noise of thunder and lightning. And the entire action of the play is built around a freak storm that has enormous consequences for all the individuals and the location. And people have heard of the play and it's got a massive weather event in its title, so that means the audience is already primed in a way they wouldn't necessarily be with *Henry IV, Part 2*.

I worry about eco-readings of Shakespeare plays which are bleak and dystopian, like the *Macbeth* hellscape that is just what we will have to cope with. To me that doesn't make an audience come out wanting to be better citizens or clear up their local area or rescue a bee next time they see it on a path. And those micro-gestures of behavioural change lead to bigger attitude changes.

In our *Tempest*, I hope audiences felt that people can change. We really leaned into the truth of forgiveness and redemption at the end. Hope is hard fought for in the play and it's agony: in the final scene it's painful to watch people come face-to-face with those who have tried to destroy their lives. But we showed that there's a pathway to hope. If we come through it together, we can find our way out.

Katie: I love the hope and forgiveness in *The Tempest* and all the late plays. I remember when we did our adaptation of *Cymbeline*, I thought about how important it is to forgive those who have hurt you. We all have to say what Posthumous says to Iachimo: 'live and deal with others better.' We can't just punish everyone who uses gas and buys plastic; we have to give each other grace.

In your production, you had me thinking about the Sebastians of the world who have hurt us, and how we might make them part of the solution rather than making them outcasts. We need everybody's skills, across political lines: all of us.

Elizabeth: It's never going to be simple, unambiguous, or uncomplex, as Shakespeare writes.

You have a further complication: How do you wrangle the location itself? Yosemite is a contested space; there are the people who've lived there for thousands of years and then this notion of the pristine wilderness and the white man arrives, and now it's this park which sort of is free for everyone but in reality, there are barriers to access.

Katie: Inasmuch as we can, we do try to address those issues, because Shakespeare sure doesn't. For our 2018 *Dream* we worked directly with a few members of the Southern Sierra Miwuk community who taught us Southern Sierra Miwuk words that we used in the production. This year we had Titania and Puck talk about how the humans now are not like the humans who have lived here before. All of our shows have references to Indigenous peoples, because all of our shows in some way are about the idea of living in balance. We talk about how for thousands of years in Yosemite, Indigenous humans and nature lived in balance. Pointing that out helps us explain that the answer to environmental problems isn't 'no humans'. Native Americans did controlled burns, they lived in balance, and the ecosystem thrived because of their presence.

Production Goals for *Dream*

Elizabeth: In your production I experienced the activation of time in a kind of temporal whiplash. There were multi-million-year-old rocks rising above the stage, and this 400-year-old play, and then this 1930s world in which the play began, which collided with the contemporary world when the rest of the play is set. What does the idea of time give you eco-dramaturgically?

Katie: It's important to think about time when we think about the climate crisis. As a species we are future-blind; we have trouble imagining our own deaths, or anything being different from what it is now. But we need to be able to imagine the future, and one way to do that is to think about the past and how decisions made in the past have consequences that we are living with now. Our audiences might not know exactly how old Shakespeare is or the precise geological history of Yosemite, but they do know that those things are old.

The 1930s story came about because of this incredible archival discovery that the great director Max Reinhardt was asked to stage a *Dream* in Yosemite in 1934, but ended up doing it in the Hollywood Bowl instead. That counterfactual, and the idea that fairies from the 1930s might encounter our present world, was the starting point for our adaptation. And once we started thinking about the 1930s, we realized that it was an era that saw the damming of rivers, the suppression of fires, and a real ramping up of tourism in National Parks. We are living with the consequences of these decisions today. We wanted spectators to think about how people who are alive 90 years from now are going to be living with the decisions we are making.

Elizabeth: You began that 1930s sequence with four fairies representing the four elements. The fire element, Oberon's element, was getting too powerful and Titania/Water, Puck/Earth, and Ariel/Air were trying to bring the world into balance. Did you see these ideas as latent in the text or did you have to look for spaces where you could tell that story?

Katie: We asked: 'Who are these people and fairies if we put them in Yosemite?' Titania and Oberon are the most powerful figures in the fairy kingdom and the fairy kingdom is an extension of the natural world. If the natural world is the Yosemite world, who are the most powerful forces? Well, the most powerful forces in Yosemite are fire and water, for both good and bad. Fire and water have shaped that park, and now fire and water are what threaten it. The park is frequently evacuated due to catastrophic forest fire, and both drought and flood are big threats to the whole Sierra ecosystem. Once we knew Oberon and Titania were fire and water, it made sense for Puck to be earth, and to import Ariel from *The Tempest* to be air.

Elizabeth: You have taken the idea of these four elements, and they have got out of balance because of the fire suppression that's been practiced in North America for the last 90 years or so.

Katie: Yes, and the thought was more fully that in the Anthropocene, human impact has gotten the natural world out of balance. Our Oberon, as the fire king, is cheering humans on: he likes that humans are harnessing fire to power automobiles and aeroplanes. Oberon's getting more powerful because of human action, but that is causing problems for the whole natural world. When we meet Oberon, he's fighting with Titania, Puck, and Ariel about this, which mirrors the brawl that begins 2.1 in Shakespeare's *Dream*.

Elizabeth: At the end of that opening scene, the fairies hide in the fire scar of a giant sequoia.

Katie: When adapting, I at first did not know what was going to happen to the 1930s fairies that was going to preserve them until 2024. Through conversation with our designer Adam, we both realized that they must go into the fire scar of a sequoia: something that's ancient, something that's thousands of years old, and something that's big enough.

Elizabeth: When the fairies are awoken in 2024, the natural world has changed.

Katie: Yes, and one of the first things they realize is that in the 90 years in which they've been hiding, fire suppression, which prevents smaller fires from keeping a landscape healthy and free of flammable brush, has led to a massive build-up of fuels, and mixed with global warming from those planes and cars, wildfires have become massive and catastrophic.

Elizabeth: Beyond the sense of deep time, something else that gave your production a sense of massive scale is the literally jaw-dropping magnificence of the backdrop in Yosemite.

Katie: A lot of environmentalists are trying to move away from the idea that nature is this thing that you must drive to get to, and that wildernesses are beautiful places where nature-lovers go to recreate that are separate from most people's lives. It's important that we think about the environment as everywhere; even if we're in a city centre, we are part of an ecosystem.

That being said, it is also true that a lot of people find that they contemplate the very idea of ecosystems and their own role in preserving life on Earth more deeply when they're in a place like Yosemite. And historically, a love of the natural world and its beauty has preserved a lot of ecosystems. When we think about a landscape's magnificence, we experience those feelings of awe that lead to being more cooperative and humble. But it's not just that public lands preserve pretty places for humans to look at; they also preserve biodiversity, trees that mitigate the climate crisis, clean waters.

Production Goals and Casting for *The Tempest*

Katie: As you were preparing your *Tempest*, what did you want your audiences to come away knowing, and what did you want them to feel?

Elizabeth: My show's different from yours in that people didn't come out of my show knowing a fact, like that 20 per cent of the world's sequoias were lost.

Katie: Can I say I think there was? If you didn't know, you learned that small island nations are at the front edge of climate catastrophe. And you also learned that ocean pollution and ocean trash are threatening ecosystems (see Figure 6).

Elizabeth: Yes, I hope that people thought about the impact of ocean pollution, and I hope what they felt was the potential for change. The physical environment completely transformed in front of their eyes from this detritus-strewn cesspit into something beautiful. And you saw that happen through humans, and via the more-than-human world, which humans helped embody. During the three hours that you watch the show, you experience positive environmental change.

Katie: Let's talk about when the play was written and how you thought about that.

Elizabeth: It's thought that Shakespeare based it on two real events that happened. One was the wreck of the Sea Venture, a British ship on an early colonizing expedition to the Caribbean. The incident speaks to the beginnings of globalization and colonization.

Then there's a story that's closer to home, which was that there were enormous floods that happened in England a couple of years before Shakespeare wrote *The Tempest*, including what scientists now say could have been categorized as a tsunami. Spring tides and freak weather coincided to bring a massive wave up the River Severn, flooding the entire Bristol Channel and swamping much of the surrounding farmland. About

Performing Shakespeare on an Endangered Planet

Figure 6 Joseph Payne as Ferdinand in *The Tempest*, Royal Shakespeare Theatre, 2023. Photo credit: Ikin Yum

3,000 people were thought to have died. It is highly likely that Shakespeare was aware of it. The Avon itself flooded throughout Shakespeare's lifetime and continues to flood today. In fact, when I was thinking about the play, the Avon was in full flood. All of what we are looking at now was underwater just a few months ago. The reality of living with the water coming over your head is present in Shakespeare's time and in ours today.

What you see in the play is people trying to survive. People are on this exposed, unforgiving island and they wrestle with how they're going to cope with it. Is it going to bring out the best of them or the worst of them? The situation forces people to be in community and figure out how to do better together. As with *Dream*, the more-than-human world is very present. There's Ariel and the spirits who are the embodiment of some kind of indigenous natural world that was there long before humans ever arrived. And Caliban is a first-generation arrival on the island before westerners took it over. It thinks about both the hyperlocal and the global and colonial impacts of the climate crisis, and it shows different kinds of humans in this extraordinary climate-induced survival situation. And then the play is set in the Mediterranean, if you are literal about the text. Today, a Mediterranean story can't *not* become a refugee narrative.

Katie: Indeed, and many of those refugees are climate refugees, that paradigmatic example of environmental injustice that stands at the intersection of colonialism and the climate crisis. For a long time, interpreting *The Tempest* through a decolonial lens has been popular. How has your thinking about colonization informed an ecological reading of the play?

Elizabeth: There have been hundreds of productions that have highlighted a very particular aspect of British history, through the othering of Caliban and having him be from any of the thousands of places where the British have had a terrible influence. We needed to eco-activate that story. Tommy, who ended up playing Caliban, is a British Iraqi actor. Through conflict and through resource exploitation, the British continue to have a very negative impact in Iraq. And in fact, over half the acting company represent the global majority, many dual nationality, from five or six non-British nationalities. They brought their lived experience to the rehearsal room and therefore into their character interpretations. The company represented all kinds of heritages, class backgrounds, and lived experiences, and the idea was to ask: 'who are we all in the face of a rising sea? Who is impacted worse by that?'

Katie: While we're talking about casting, I want to think also about gender.

Elizabeth: We've been talking about eco-racism, the idea that most of the people who are on the front line of the climate crisis are those least responsible for causing the droughts and hurricanes that are harming them. Within that, women are more likely to feel the impacts of the climate crisis because of the places that they live and because of their involvement in domestic tasks that often involve water and washing and needing to be near some kind of clean water source. In any extreme situation, it's usually women who end up being exploited, be that through rape and sexual assault or through poverty or having more caring responsibilities.

To speak to that I wanted a mother-daughter dynamic at the heart of the story (see Figure 5). It became clear that as Miranda grows up, Prospero must think about what's going to happen to her next. Prospero, Miranda, and Caliban had all lived very happily together; we are told that three times in the play. The kids hit adolescence and Caliban's grown into somebody who's physically very strong and now sexual, and that threat is the instigating incident for Prospero. She needs to get Miranda off this island; there's no way that she can stay here. That's how a parent would think in that situation. That is the dynamic that we tried to evoke in the hope that it would speak to the female experience in climate-traumatic times.

Lived Realities and Casting *Dream*

Katie: I was touched when you talked about how the climate crisis is affecting your home here in Stratford, and what it's like to look at a flooded river. I know that feeling these crises for ourselves motivates both of us. In the process of doing *Dream*, I experienced wildfire smoke and was able to see wildfires glow in the Sierra from where I live; the year before, it was catastrophic flooding that destroyed homes in Merced.

Elizabeth: Exactly, it's a lived reality. This work is not just academic, it is not in the realm of theory, it is in the real here and now and therefore in our audience's here and now. These things are part of our everyday lived experiences and they're only going to become more so.

Katie: In Stratford you're performing for people who have lived through floods and seen them, and in Yosemite we are performing for actual fire personnel, and folks who have evacuated due to fires. They are reliving these experiences as they see our shows.

Elizabeth: That was clear to me when watching your show: people were genuinely moved when the sequoias were referenced. I saw people shake their heads or a tear fall. It was an extraordinary moment when Oberon sang to the lost sequoias. It was sort of devastating. The emotional power came from connecting an old play from the other side of the world and activating it to speak to something so present and important.

But I want to ask you about your casting. Your approach to non-gender-normative casting seems to be about actively breaking a system, of getting past patriarchal structures and presenting a world that can be more than human, and can be gender identifying in whatever form it wants to be.

Katie: Shakespeare, as person and concept, can be used to uphold the patriarchy, and that's the opposite of what we want to do and the opposite of what we *need* to do as a society to create a more just world. We were thinking both socially and ecologically about how we make sure that women have at least as much power as men. And as you were saying, we also acknowledged that it's women and people of colour who are at the front lines of these environmental crises. Mary Robinson's book (2018) has highlighted that it's often women and people of colour who are at the front lines of the *solutions*, and we highlighted that.

We are aware that we're dealing with two worlds, the Shakespearean stage and the so-called American wilderness, that are traditionally domains of white men. When people think of wilderness and who goes there, when they think of a park ranger or a firefighter or even a climber, they think of a white man first. Making sure that people of colour and women and queer people feel comfortable in both of those worlds and celebrating their contributions is always important in our shows. We are also inspired by the work of the drag queen Patty Gonia who is really thinking about making sure that queer people in both rural and wilderness spaces are celebrated: nature is for everyone.

Beyond that, because we're doing comedies it also becomes a related question of who gets to love. I was really moved that I had several queer students say that having a female Lysandra and a Hermia that were clearly so happy in the end helped them feel more hopeful about their own futures (see Figure 7).

Elizabeth: My experience of that was that it was doubly powerful. Because it's this queer, positive story inside a Shakespeare play, which is an unexpected place to find it. For your average audience member, that's surprising, and then those humans speak the language of love that Shakespeare writes so beautifully. I was watching that story in a bastion of what I assumed to be white, male American hiker-land. Just a few yards away from where you did the show, there's a shop selling hiking gear and

Performing Shakespeare on an Endangered Planet 49

Figure 7 Madelyn Lara as Hermia and Mia Hinshaw as Lysandra in *Misdummer Yosemite's Dream*. UC Merced campus, 2024. Photo credit: Amirhadi Shirzadibonab.

it's just got photos of white guys hanging off cliffs, half of them with their tops off. Your love story between Lysandra and Hermia was another layer of welcome and another gesture of subversion. *Dream* is sort of brilliant at representing both relationship love and friendship love.

Working with Shakespeare's Language

Elizabeth: Do you feel that there's something inherently spacious or elastic inside Shakespeare's texts that allows them to be the right vehicle?

Katie: I think the complexity and the spaciousness of the language mimics the complexity and the spaciousness of the natural world. The imaginative leaps it takes to imagine *Dream*'s fairy world prepare one to think expansively. But speaking of complex language, I want you to talk about what was to me a highlight of the play: Alex Kingston's delivery of the 'our revels now are ended' speech.

Elizabeth: That speech became about the generational gap between baby boomers and younger generations. Prospero is watching her daughter in a new relationship, beginning her adult life. And Prospero suddenly realizes that her generation messed it up, like absolutely kind of destroyed it, and the façade crumbles. She can't pretend anymore that we can have this gorgeous glory of singing and dancing and warmth of the masque, because that's not the world we made. And then she has a vision of what that world really is.[26]

Alex delivered it as if she could see the cloud-capped towers and the palaces, a cityscape. The London or the New York skylines are empty promises to future generations, temples of hubris and the folly of human exceptionalism. And when she said 'the great Globe itself', she realized that it's going to be destroyed, all of that is going to go. That vision gave her a perspective on what had happened in the past. Looking into the future, she could see what that was going to mean for her daughter and her daughter's daughter.

Katie: That for me was one of the most profound and powerful moments not just of that production, but that I've ever experienced in the theatre. And not a word of Shakespeare was changed. Was that something you thought of when preparing the production, or did the two of you come up with it together?

Elizabeth: We very much came up with it together. I knew that Act 4 with the masque was going to be where I would make eco-dramaturgical sense of the entire production (see Figure 8). Prospero suddenly stops all the singing and dancing because she remembers that Caliban is coming to kill her. Then from that, she goes into this extraordinary speech. I knew that navigating that section would be key to making the eco-messaging of the play really land.

I also knew that I didn't want to change it. I sensed that it was there in the text. Academics write about the masque as an in-joke, Shakespeare doing a Ben Jonson thing. But I trust Shakespeare and I thought 'hang on,

---

[26] For an eerily similar reading of this speech, see Charles McNulty's reflections on how these lines from *The Tempest* were in his head as he witnessed the LA fires (2025).

Figure 8 Liz Jadav, Imogen Slaughter, and Natalia Campbell as Sky, Earth, and Rain in *The Tempest*. Costume design Tom Piper and Natasha Ward. Royal Shakespeare Theatre, 2023. Photo Credit: Ikin Yum

isn't this him actually writing about the world that could be and the world that should be on this island? That it shouldn't just be a ravaged ecosystem here?' It was really clear to me straightaway that this was thematically the point of the play, and not just a separate play within a play.

The only thing that I felt was really alien to the audience was calling the goddesses their Roman names. Intervention number one was to adjust their names. Juno is the goddess of the sky and Ceres is the goddess of the earth and Iris is the messenger goddess of water and rain and rainbows. So the moment we thought of them as Rain, Earth, and Sky, they become elemental figures who have genuinely come to help. They realize that these young people are Generation Greta [Thunberg], and that we need to nurture them and let their love nurture this sapling.

Renaming the goddesses meant that Prospero could find herself in a completely different mindset. The goddesses deliver her an extraordinary vision, and she comes out of that and knows absolutely what the state of the world is and will be. We did a big improvisation of that moment in week 1 and Alex was just watching Jess (Miranda) and Joe (Ferdinand) do this beautiful love improv to music. She started crying and then she found herself being furious. And then she was clear about how she needed to do the speech. We tried not to over-rehearse it. She as a human genuinely feels that so that's not a big imaginative leap.

But you are much looser with the text than me. When you actually look at the textual material, what are your adaptive lodestars?

Katie: I wanted to think about living in balance, and relatedly, fire. So I went through and cut a lot, and decided which lines are going to be particularly highlighted, which lines are going to be altered, always thinking about how to tell this environmental story while also telling the actual story of *Dream*.

Elizabeth: Do you find it quite an easy process to just excise?

Katie: Yes. A lot of speeches in Shakespeare, what you need to know comes fairly early in the speech and then the character just keeps talking. So when we get rid of the 'just keeps talking part', the dialogue is a lot easier for audiences to understand.

Elizabeth: Tell me more about how you rearranged those opening scenes to establish the travel between 1934 and 2024, and how you worked with Titania's speech about the seasons altering.

Katie: We divided up act 2 scene 1 so that part of act 2 scene 1 came at the beginning of the play. The first part of act 2 scene 1, set in 1934, introduced the fact that there was fighting between Oberon and Titania and that they hid in the fire scar of the Sequoia with Puck and Ariel until the humans might listen. Then came 1.1 and 1.2, set in the present, where we introduce the lovers and the Mechanicals. When we continued act 2 scene 1, it started with the plant and animal fairies of 2024 who had been living with the consequences of human interventions for 90 years, and they reunited with the elemental fairies. They had a lot to tell them about what has happened in the last 90 years: one of them, Red-Legged Frog, had almost gone extinct and was brought back by humans. We told the stories of humans both hurting and helping the natural world.

Those 2024 fairies began the delivery of Titania's climate change speech (2.1.84–120), and they divided up and acted it out physically with their bodies. They tried desperately to convey climate change's consequences to the natural world and the human world. The humans are starving, and they have lost their winter cheer. They were giving this speech and Titania immediately understood: 'this is exactly what I predicted 90 years ago.' She joined in and finished it: 'and this same progeny of evils comes from our debate from our dissension/We are their parents and original'. We have neglected our duty to keep looking after this world. We have let powerful humans get out of control.

Elizabeth: You had a positive story of human intervention, the reintroduction of the red-legged frog, and I found it impactful that that success story was built into this moment, while the fairies are revealing the extent of damage from fires and everything else.

And then walked in a group of Mechanicals, who are actual Rangers, who effectively are on the frontlines of both of those things, dealing with the worst impacts as well as being involved in these success stories.[27] There was something about having them on stage that allowed the audience to keep both those thoughts in their mind: the destruction and the success.

Katie: There are so many people who are working against the kind of greed and extraction that is leading to these problems. And a lot of our audience are people who work in Yosemite and we want them to feel seen and appreciated.

Elizabeth: The biggest bit of textual adaptation that we did in *The Tempest* was some rewriting around the masque. We added in a little bit of Sonnet 65, a little bit of Sonnet 94, and a little bit of Sonnet 123. Within one of those we added in the iconic line you've just discussed from Titania's forgeries of jealousy speech about the mazéd world. I know that you also had some bits of *Tempest* in your show.

---

[27] Rangers are US National Park Service and National Forest Service employees who maintain trails, protect fragile ecosystems, and inform and guide the public in the US public parks, sites, and lands. In February 2025, while we were doing final revisions, the presidential administration fired thousands of NPS and NFS rangers, some of the country's most vital and dedicated civil servants.

Katie: I think that Shakespeare's late plays give us such a wonderful template for thinking about the forgiveness that is necessary to really work together as a society on the climate crisis. There isn't really a moment like that in *Dream*, but Shakespeare put it in *The Tempest* and I've always loved those lines where Prospero realizes that 'the rarer action is in virtue than in vengeance' (5.1.35). Prospero came to that because a nonhuman figure, Ariel, says 'I would [have empathy] were I human' (5.1.26). I wanted to import that into the play in the moment where Titania realizes that Oberon, who has not been listening, now gets it. He saw the sequoias that he thought were indestructible; 20 per cent of them are gone. Instead of saying 'I was right,' Titania needs to forgive him. Rewriting that Ariel and Prospero bit as a conversation between Titania and Puck ended up working well and gave us something that Shakespeare had given us, he just hadn't given us in that play.

Adapting beyond Language

Elizabeth: This is a lot of subtle and complicated stuff to share with an audience while telling the plot of a Shakespeare play at the same time. You do that through a mixture of contemporary language, music, and Shakespearean text. Do you need that mix to be able to activate these many ideas?

Katie: Yes, and we realized that when we did our first *Dream*, which did not change the text very much. We wanted that show to be about over-consumption and we thought we were being clear. When we asked people what they learned about the show in audience surveys, they said, 'I learned not to litter.' We realized that our conceptualizing wasn't doing what we needed it to do and adjusted accordingly. Every year we get bolder with the adaptation because we care more about the planet than we care about Shakespeare.

I should also say that our audiences are very different from RSC audiences. These are not people who woke up that morning thinking they'd be seeing *any* play that day: they're probably anticipating a hike. Many have never seen Shakespeare before. And they can get up and leave at any time. So the hybrid nature of our shows – the music, the new lines, the narrators – all that is playing to outdoor audiences who are primarily folks who are more interested in Yosemite than Shakespeare, but whose interest in Shakespeare has usually grown by the time the show is over.

I think of our added lines and music as extra-Shakespearean, not anti-Shakespearean. When you combine Shakespeare and Yosemite and ecological thought, what arises from it is new creativity.

Elizabeth: How do you make the musical choices?

Katie: I've long believed in the power of music to, in a positive but not coercive way, unite audience members who might feel differently about things. There's a reason that music is used in marches and was such a big part of the Civil Rights Movement. Music can bring out the emotional and resilient best in people.

Often one of the first things that happen in our adaptive processes is that we have a shared playlist and we're adding songs to it, particularly my music director Tonatiuh Newbold and me (see Figure 9). With James Taylor's 'Fire and Rain', I suddenly thought about that in terms of the sequoias and started crying. It wasn't that I was looking for a song for Oberon to sing, but rather that thinking about that song and the loss of the sequoias prompted that whole plot point. I always want there to be ecological grief in our shows: it is important to me that we let people grieve the losses to the planet, because the grief is part of our love, and that motivates us (see also brown, 2023: 157).

So music develops plot during the writing process. But also, there's something about singing '500 Miles' with a bunch of Park Rangers and perfect strangers and just being a little bit silly that opens you up to be more generous and vulnerable. That happened in our production, and then we end with a Harry Belafonte song that refers to fire and water and mountains and brings everyone on stage. Different generations, people who look different, people who are representing the nonhuman, all pledge through song to 'Turn the World Around'. And because you've already been singing along, you're implied in that final moment.

In terms of music choice the students often ask 'why are we singing this Marvin Gaye or Simon and Garfunkel song?' We do have some songs from the twenty-first century, but the older songs, a lot of younger generations know them, but your average sixty-year-old might not know Chappell Roan.

Elizabeth: I wonder if they also do that thing of activating time again. It was so moving when you had the Paul Simon duet in your show, the 'Sound of Silence/American Tune' montage when Hermia and Helena were lost in the

Figure 9 Tonatiuh Newbold as Oberon. Costume design by Mahea LaRosa and Grace Garnica. *Midsummer Yosemite's Dream*, Yosemite National Park, 2024. Photo Credit: Grace Garnica

woods singing these tracks of the '60s and '70s, because it became about their own modern eco-anxiety. You were aware of that generational gap, from that beautiful promise of that '60s protest time, what the world could have been.

Katie: Absolutely, and that was a particularly profound part of our *Love's Labour's Lost* in 2022, which was set in 1969. Every song in that show was from that moment, the protests that led to the early '70s environmental legislation. Having Gen Z kids sing those John Lennon and Joni Mitchell songs to Boomers who remembered them and remembered that they used to fight for these things was profound. Younger Generations were able to say, 'you fought for this stuff that we're fighting for', and older Generations were able to remember that they did that. We recognized that power, so in our *Romeo and Juliet* and *Dream* we continue to use some older songs that activate those memories of being a teenager. You're never more idealistic than when you're a teenager. So having songs from different decades activates that youthful hope for multiple audience members.

In calling for what he calls 'existential creativity' Ben Okri says that 'it is now time for us to be the most creative we have ever been, the most farsighted, the most practical, the most conscious and selfless' (2021). This section has outlined how to ecologically adapt Shakespeare through hopeful play selection; intentional goals and inclusive team building; textual cutting and emendation; and finding accessible ways to enliven productions. In the next section, we discuss how design, construction, and rehearsal processes might work in harmony with these aims.

3 Eco-Practices, or, How to Make Shakespeare Plays That Don't Cost the Earth

'And this our life ... finds tongues in tree, books in running brooks, sermons in stones, and good in everything' (*As You Like It* 1.2.15–17)

'The ultimate, hidden truth of the world, is that it is something we make, and could just as easily make differently' – David Graeber (2015, 89)

This section focuses on the process of making a Shakespeare play ecological both on and off stage. Una Chaudhuri has long called for theatre-making practices that couple environmental narratives with resource-aware practices, that is, attention to the environmental impact of physically producing a show (1994). When it comes to creating a production that addresses environmental issues in the *on*-stage narrative, using sustainable *off*-stage production processes double down on the impact. These are practices that don't cost the earth – in any sense, for what is ecological is also economical. This is the case whether productions take place inside, outside, online, or on the move, and it is via those four types of production that this section is organized:

I. Inside: considering design and selecting materials
II. Outside: embracing weather and practicing stewardship
III. On the move: reaching audiences and projecting forward
IV. Online: connecting communities and disseminating best practice

After describing eco-practices relating to each of these production environments, the section concludes with a discussion between Elizabeth and Katie about how they made their respective productions of *The Tempest* and *Midsummer Night's Dream*.

3.1 Taking Material Care

Theatre-making has traditionally been a high-resource industry, often involving the construction and disposal of enormous sets made of timber and steel, power draining lights, booming sound systems, and fast fashion or single-use bespoke costumes made from scratch. Companies order props online, fast-delivered for next-day rehearsals and corral audiences into buying programmes, mass produced merchandise, and drinks in plastic cups. When the run of the show is finished, most of these materials are thrown away as the company starts again on the next production. The process is both wasteful and costly (see Garrett, 2012).

Thankfully, there's help at hand. The Theatre Green Book began as a shared endeavour by a group of UK theatre makers to champion environmentally minded theatre-making and has since grown into a global initiative, advocating for the industry to become more sustainable 'through common language, actions, and standards that allow us to share and learn together' (2024: 2). This free online resource contains a set of guiding principles, actionable advice, monitoring templates, case studies, toolkits, and training, with adaptable frameworks for differing scales and contexts. Other green theatre-making endeavours are mobilizing artists and companies to turn a high-waste resource-intensive industry into a zero-waste business, including Julie's Bicycle, Broadway Green Alliance, The Center for Sustainable Practice in the Arts, and Ecostage (see Appendix C for websites for all these organizations and others). There are many others, and surely more to come.

So where does Shakespeare fit into all this green creativity?

Shakespeare's plays can be particularly resource intensive. Large casts require more bodies to costume, often in multiple outfits. Wondrous moments such as reveals and surprises ask for the delivery of spectacle. Blood and gore, disguises and parties, fairies and soldiers, shipwrecks and heaths: the thrilling dramatic set-pieces that make Shakespeare so endlessly appealing seem to require material realization on stage. What that equates to is an aftermath of waste: broken fairy wings and a bulging bear suit next to a rusty sword and a witch's hat; a Shakespearean rubbish heap full of *stuff*.

That use of stuff, however, is antithetical to how many scholars suggest Shakespeare's plays were originally presented: on an uncluttered, naturally lit, outdoor stage with handheld props, reusable (even personally owned) costumes, and live music, or, later, indoors, lit by candles.[28] With limited funds and high prices on fabrics and other materials, thrift, creativity, and pragmatism combined to make for what would today be called a reduce/reuse/recycle aesthetic. This section is not a call to return to original Shakespearean practices (we like women on the stage, thank you very much), but does suggest that taking inspiration from early modern approaches to material care helps us limit the damage that productions can do.

When Shakespeare asks the audience, through the voice of the Chorus in *Henry V*, to 'think when we talk of horses, that you see them', he is celebrating the 'imaginary forces' that spectators are required to summon to enter the performers' pretend world (Prologue.27). Asking the audience to do this imaginative work, as we have seen in Section 1, is a key component of turning passive spectatorship into active witness. And Brand Shakespeare gives the theatre-maker an imaginative head-start. Audiences come primed to fill in the gaps, ready to accept earthbound fairies, full armies represented by a handful of actors, and dead bodies that

---

[28] Amongst many volumes on early modern theatre practices see, for example Karim-Cooper and Stern (2013).

appear to miraculously get up and walk off the stage. Theatre-makers can dare to use as little as possible to make as much as possible; in other words, to use their own 'imaginary forces' and take the creative gauntlet laid down by the demands of the plays as an eco-theatrical challenge.

As we discussed in Section 1, assembling a team with diverse lived experiences and skill sets is essential: an eco-hive mind can problem-solve the demands of the play in light of environmental impact. The focus becomes both the world of the play and the precious world in which we live. Here are a few of the many ways that theatre-makers might choose to go about rising to this challenge:

1) Re-invent the performance space
2) Make no waste
3) Create with community
4) Pay it forward

Where companies perform dictates much of their carbon footprint in terms of resources and energy. It also impacts who feels welcomed into the performance space and how likely the audience might be to feel empowering 'microprogressions'. More equitable performer/audience dynamics better empower audiences. For example, Maine, USA's Recycled Shakespeare Company is a grassroots community organization whose ethos is 'to build communities through green theatre-making' (Fournier, 2020). Their free, low-tech productions take place in pop-up civic spaces: *Romeo and Juliet* in a pizza restaurant, *Macbeth* in a church hall, and *Richard III* in a disused cinema.

When it comes to the design process, companies can anticipate, calculate, and negate their resource use to comply with ecological principles, a practice Tanja Beer calls 'ecoscenography' (2021). They can use existing materials found in storage or borrow and rent (surely every Shakespeare company has a skull and some ass's ears?). They can make the rest out of found objects: a crafty approach to making can provide a positive material connection to both early modern theatre-making (look at the Mechanicals in *A Midsummer Night's Dream*, divvying up the sourcing of their props and working out how to present 'wall') and to the company's own physical connections with *stuff* (see Figures 10 and 11).

Performing Shakespeare on an Endangered Planet 61

Figure 10 Designer Miranda Cruz fits a costume for Parnassian (Joanna Lopez) for *A Midsummer Yosemite's Dream*. Photo credit: Katherine Steele Brokaw

This work need not be solely the responsibility of the designers: the entire team can be in active dialogue with the material world of the production; everyone can save their shiny yoghurt tops to make Moonshine's vest, for example. The aforementioned Recycled Shakespeare Company (aka, the alternative RSC) takes the mantra 'reduce, reuse, recite'. They have what their founder, the late Emily Fournier, called 'the six-inch rule . . . if it has six inches of usable spaces, we hold onto it and we use it' (qtd. in Brokaw, 2023a: 263). They collect and store rubbish, and embrace the creative ingenuity that assorted junk and jumble requires a company to bring to the production.

Figure 11 Marcy Poe Martinez and Sofia Andom as Puck and Titania, wearing reused, thrifted, and made-from-trash costumes. Costume design by Mahea LaRosa. *A Midsummer Yosemite's Dream*, Yosemite National Park, 2024. Photo credit: Grace Garnica

These kinds of processes can also activate on-stage items to help tell an environmental story. Recycled objects enable new meaningful connections between today's 'stuff' and Shakespeare's world. For example, making fairy wings from rubbish (as in Katie's production of *Dream*) speaks subtly to the impact of plastic pollution on the more-than-human world. Making the reuse of materials visible to the audience lets the eco-significance of a prop or design choice contribute to the ecodramaturgical meaning of a production. This also avoids the aestheticization of rubbish, instead using visual iconography as a powerful communication tool. A Recycled Shakespeare Company production of *Richard III* used hubcaps found on roadsides as shields, an effective piece of recycling in its own right, but also one in which the supposedly protective shields were sourced from something (cars) that has caused as much destruction to people and planet as the conflicts in the play. Hubcaps also appeared in previous productions including *Macbeth*, inviting audiences to read across narratives and draw links between repeated actions and behaviours. Writing of how early modern theatre-makers similarly often re-used the same props, Elizabeth E. Tavares et al. propose that 'this recycling of objects might prompt an affective response from the audiences of multiple plays in repertory, whose memory of one play creates the opportunity to connect images and meanings to another' (2023: 5).[29]

All of the aforementioned can be done by collaborating with audiences and communities: doing call-outs for required items or materials, setting up local research events to better understand specific environmental concerns, and working with local charity shops, schools, and businesses. All co-creation practice builds engagement, makes the work more specific and personal, and reaches new audiences.[30] Theatre can thus contribute to community-building, not just as a side benefit but as a vital aspect of eco-theatre: sociologists have found that community participation, particularly from community-based organizations and labour unions, is one of the most effective ways to combat climate change (Almeida et al., 2023).

Finally, companies can pay it forward. They can take the money saved by not paying author royalties and redirect it to local environments. Flagstaff Shakespeare has redirected some of its profits to benefit local

---

[29] See also Carlson, 2003, which documents the intentionality of recycled stage objects for theatrical effect as well as Duncan, 2019 and Perkins, 2010.

[30] Useful theoretical grounding for this practice can be found in Horvath and Carpenter, 2020 and Walmsley, 2013. See also O'Shea, 2011 on arts engagement with sustainable communities.

water health. Or companies can volunteer their time to help with local clean-ups and disaster reliefs, as Theatricum Botanicum – near the worst of the 2025 Palisades fires – has done several times. Giving nature a royalty through money or sweat equity acknowledges the unspoken gift of Shakespeare being royalty free.

3.2 Outside: Playing the Rain

There is a long tradition of outdoor Shakespeare performance, from Shakespeare's Globe in London to the Shakespeare in the Park tradition that Joseph Papp began in Central Park in the 1950s, versions of which can be found in venues across North America. People are pretty used to the idea of Shakespeare productions happening in parks and green spaces and even in forests and on beaches. Performers and audiences being in shared meteorological conditions makes for a democratized production experience. Theresa J. May further argues that any form of non-traditional staging induces deeper levels of engagement as it 'deconstructs the separation between audience and actor, and produces new levels of audience participation and reciprocation' (2005: 96).

Production teams can be intentional about drawing attention to place and weather, making the performing environment part of the play's meaning. An indoor production can use lights and set to conjure a sweltering sun or heavy grey bleakness. Outside, however, the weather and the place will be what the weather and place actually are, and production teams must choose if and whether (*sic*) to respond to the actual, live environmental conditions the cast and audience are experiencing or to stick to the words as written and allow the gap – if there is one – between actual and fictional realities to be visible.

Una Chaudhuri claims that theatre is 'programmatically anti-ecological', citing a long-standing tendency for artists and audiences to interpret any representation of environmental circumstances as merely backstory to human action, or a metaphor for human struggles (1994: 24). For example, the forest in *As You Like It* might simply be seen as a benign, passive backdrop to the action, or the storm in *King Lear* just a manifestation of the title character's inner distress. But environments are not merely spaces for humans to navigate, or representations of their feelings – they have their own agency and actively affect all inhabitants. So how do theatre-makers activate place and weather to be not just legible, but also an agential and decisive part of the plot? Here are some ways that theatre-makers can rise to this challenge:

1) Be where you are
2) Eco-adopt the elements
3) Practice stewardship
4) Situate the geography of difference

Place is a holder of history and environmental legacy. By speaking to the reality of the location where the production takes place, companies can amplify local environmental concerns and expose the gap between historical issues and those of today. This reconstitutes theatre as a site of civic discourse, asking the audience to notice their own presence in a particular location. This might mean placing a dystopian world on stage within a wider environment of natural beauty, letting the narrative be antithetical to the outdoor backdrop. Or, it could mean referencing what is in the audience's eyeline directly within the action of the play, whether that be a mansion house, a tree, or as in Montana InSite's production of *Timon of Anaconda*, a former industrial site (see Minton, 2021). Productions can acknowledge local biodiversity through engagement with references to flora and fauna in the play, animating local nature in conversation with the text. These gestures make the work place-specific rather than existing in an atemporal, apolitical, other-world. Productions become localized and audience-specific, increasing the chances of the audience finding personal entry-points into the world of the play.

Performing outdoors gives theatre-makers the opportunity to eco-adapt to the environment in all its variety. The moon, the sun, and the stars can be called upon, cursed, prayed to, or raged at. Human-scale narratives can appear dwarfed by the vastness of the skies, placing anthropogenic existence in a perspectival timeline of overall life on earth. There might be large-scale natural landscapes in view, like waterways or mountain tops. Eco-referencing these majesties (or making clear their lack of visibility due to light or other pollution, or calling attention to the state of their environmental health) encourages this kind of scalar view. Disruptions from the noisy road or airplane become part of the action of the show. Finally, there is the difference between daily, local weather and the vast, global climate experience. Productions can draw the audience's attention to the difference between these by acknowledging the unseasonability, or the 'distemperature', of a changing world in the place where it is being performed.

Outdoor shows risk damaging local environments and contributing to noise and light pollution. Importing productions, with their associated material and technological elements, and bringing audiences *en masse* to a place not necessarily designated for that purpose can lead to fleeting or lasting environmental damage. The first rule of outdoor Shakespeare is to take care of the ecosystem in which it is performed and leave no trace. Companies can even improve the lands on which they perform with a litter pick or sapling donation. See Appendix A for examples of the way many Shakespeare companies from the Willow Globe in Wales to Santa Cruz Shakespeare make neutral or positive impacts on their outdoor venues by relying on natural light and sustainable equipment and asking audiences to engage with green practices like recycling and composting.

Finally, act locally, but think globally. Shakespeare is performed all over the world, in all kinds of contexts. An English history play might get performed on a Caribbean beach. A Roman tragedy can unfold in an African city park. A global perspective to a localized production asks the audience to draw their own links between peoples and places, between Shakespeare's time and today's.

3.3 Making the Journey Part of the Destination

Touring Shakespeare reaches back to the days of Elizabethan travelling players packing swords and hats into a bag and setting off to provincial market towns on a well-trodden players circuit (Somerset, 1994). This was especially the case during the plagues of 1593 and 1594, when London theatres were closed for fear of mass transmission of disease in publicly crowded places. However, touring productions today generate carbon emissions through the movement of people and the physical components of the production across regions, counties, or the world. Each production must weigh up the potentially positive outcome of a show's presence versus the potentially negative impact that its method of getting there may incur.

The Theatre Green Book offers advice for greening touring practices. These include delineating haulage volumes, minimizing packing and packaging, and setting carbon budgets to limit transportation. Researching everything from local material supplies to venues' energy sources can reduce unwanted emissions and minimize what needs to travel, as can mapping a tour to minimize mileage. In addition, companies can partner with receiving venues or host organizations who follow like-minded production methodologies. Here are some ways, by no means exclusive or exhaustive, that Shakespearean theatre-makers might choose to go about rising to the challenge of green touring:

1) Storytell the journey
2) Create space for debate
3) Re-root in each place
4) Time travel into the future

How a production travels can become part of its ecological story. For example, The Handlebards are a cycling Shakespeare company who tour the UK carrying all items of set, props, and costumes required for their shows on the backs of their bikes.[31] These in turn often feature in their shows; a recent *The Comedy of Errors* used bicycle power to comic effect, thus drawing the audience's attention to the method of the company's transportation as well its role in the on-stage action. Chesapeake Shakespeare has a touring wagon with built-in lighting and sound systems that are run by solar rechargeable batteries. For their production of *A Midsummer Night's Dream*, which toured underserved communities across Baltimore, the wagon doubled as the Mechanicals' retiring house. Additionally, productions can invite audiences to think about their own travel impact by using marketing, programme notes, signage, and social media to articulate ideas of sustainable travel by encouraging public transportation, carpooling, and active travel.[32]

---

[31] The Handlebards are one of a few eco-touring companies, inspired by the now defunct Otesha Project, a cycling Canadian theatre company.

[32] For useful definitions and ideas relating to active travel see Cook et al., 2022

They can even offer discounts to people using those methods, as well as signpost audiences to changes they are making themselves, as The Rude Mechanicals do. This company performs off-grid in rural locations and now proudly power their shows with EcoFlow batteries.[33]

A word of warning: the more a company puts its head above the parapet in announcing its environmental values, the more the naysayers line up to point out all the things it's *not* doing. If a company decides it's worth flying a cast from one place to another to perform – because the benefits of doing so collectively outweigh the negative impacts of the associated carbon footprint – they can articulate that decision. There are multiple green travel calculators that compute which flights/routes/carriers produce the fewest emissions, as well as options for negating those through other actions.[34] For example, the (UK) RSC's abridged *Twelfth Night* in 2022, part of their First Encounters with Shakespeare initiative, toured town halls, schools and arts venues across England, all in areas that are underserved by funded arts and culture. It clocked up substantial diesel mileage through transporting the set and cast, but reaching young audiences and their families with a production built from visibly recycled set and costumes, alongside freely disseminated digital learning resources which explained the sustainable production process, was judged to be the bigger picture win.

The International Panel on Climate Change advocates for local communities as the cornerstone of environmental planning to mitigate the worst of the impacts on the climate crisis, arguing those on the ground in any given context are best placed to offer and enact solutions (Denton et al., 2014: 1119–1123). Each new location on tour offers a learning opportunity for the company to understand a particular place's specific environmental concerns and to seek ways to engage and offer creative acknowledgement

---

[33] For an academic account of storytelling a Shakespeare production's journey, see Minton and Gray, 2022 about Montana Shakespeare in the Park's touring eco-*Cymbeline*.

[34] The Theatre Green Book (2024) has spreadsheets that calculate emissions based on mileage/method/fuel information. The ICAO Carbon Emissions Calculator is the United Nations official tool to quantify air travel Co2E equivalence (ICAO Carbon Emissions Calculator, 2025).

and even redress in the production. This might mean re-writing a word or a few lines to allow a moment in the production to speak sympathetically to local understanding, or partnering with a particular community group or sustainable business in each location. Montana InSite Theatre tours productions across parks, forests, and former industrial sites, reworking texts into immersive experiences that encourage audience members to consider the vital role that the nonhuman world plays in their community.

Finally, theatre-makers can tour into the future of their imaginations, taking responsibility for sponsors, partners, and the afterlife of the materials. Environmental theatre-making means researching the social and environmental practices of companies from which materials are procured, and being wary of Shakespeare-related greenwashing, whereby unscrupulous companies seek positive cultural connections with the biggest brand name in theatre.[35] It means understanding the moral implications of financial sponsorship from businesses and organizations whose activities may be linked to atmospheric pollution, and knowing what will be done with a production's materials once the show is over. Cradle to cradle processes are becoming common in industrial design processes; if large global companies are able to think in these terms, why not theatre-making?[36] 'What legacy shall I bequeath to thee?' asks Lucrece in Shakespeare's poem (l. 1242), and theatre companies can ask the same.

3.4 Online Is Not Alone

The Covid pandemic's peak in 2020 led to an upsurge of a new kind of theatrical experience: online drama. With more bio-pandemics predicted as humankind's destruction of wild habitats continues apace (more human-animal contact increases animal-to-human disease transmission), perhaps the future of Shakespeare productions might be more likely to be found online. As Erin Sullivan has shown, digital Shakespeare productions might be shaped as filmed stage productions, made-for-TV performances, games, podcasts, steered social media interactions, or many other new narrative forms (2022).

---

[35] For more on artwashing, see Evans, 2015.
[36] See, for example, Michael Braungart McDonough, 2002 and Weetman, 2020.

This might seem like a sustainable form of theatre-making, but the energy and water usage for websites and marketing, ticketing software, high-res imagery, video dissemination, cloud storage, social media communication, and AI – especially generative AI – are hidden but high environmental costs (Berners-Lee, 2020). We encourage all online theatre-makers to utilize green digital technologies, like the search engine Ecosia, and disseminate work responsibly. There are manifold tools to calculate and understand your digital footprint, using green analytics to track your output.[37] What one gains from online work is the potential to reach people who otherwise would not have physical access to a production due to personal circumstances, geography, or time. An advantage of the work being out of copyright is that it can be digitally accessible. Online theatre can be a forum where people cross-reference their own immediate circumstances with those manifesting on screen, in conversation with fellow audience-members around the world. Here are some ways that theatre-makers might choose to go about engaging with the digital:

1) Eco-innovate
2) Pair form with content
3) Think big
4) Initiate dialogue

The eco-imaginative possibilities of where Shakespeare meets the online world are endless. Unhindered by geography, weather, or material creation, productions can leverage technology in manifold ways to provide audience-led opportunities for Shakespeare engagement. Online innovation can reach those who might not otherwise find the plays (or the writer) relatable, desirable, or accessible. For example, The Under Presents: *Tempest* is a multiplayer virtual reality game and online performance space loosely based on *The Tempest* (Tender Claws, 2019). Part interactive film, part co-operative video game, player-audiences move through various stages of experience on Prospero and Miranda's island that combine live, pre-recorded, and player-controlled interactions.

---

[37] See Green Digital Action, 2025, a resource from the United Nations.

Performing Shakespeare on an Endangered Planet

Matching a production's ecological themes to the most appropriate digital form allows audiences not only to enjoy the story but also to reflect on their experience. Creation Theatre's live-action *Macbeth*, first developed in 2020, takes place in a closed theatre, where three witches stage-manage what happens to Macbeth and Lady Macbeth, two people trapped in a kind of Truman-show nightmare-reality. Audiences watch the show at home via Zoom, silent solo witnesses to a tragedy whose outcome they are unable to influence, invited to ponder the consequences of inaction.

Can we connect more of the planet's people to each other, and to the environmental themes of the work? Shakespeare, as we may have already mentioned, is a big deal in most places in the world. Curious audiences, students who might not otherwise have access to the work in performance, isolated people, first-timers, enthusiastic but housebound superfans, late-night browsers: all of these people might be accessing this work in one form or another. 2020's The Show Must Go Online, for example, was an initiative to perform the whole Shakespearean canon by presenting 'a progressive vision for the future of theatre in a time of crisis'. It utilized a cast and crew of more than 500 creatives from 60 countries, resulting in a connected and creative global community. The endeavour was community-based and volunteer- and values-led, creating and holding space for underrepresented artists as well as participants of all levels of experience, with amateurs and students sharing the stage with veterans of the West End and Broadway. The whole output is available for free (The Show Must Go Online, 2020). There are multiple places where one can access other existing productions, both free and pay-walled: Shakespeare's Globe has an online production bank; RSC and other productions are available to view via Digital Theatre; MIT has a global production archive (MIT Global Shakespeare Project, 2024); and many companies upload their work on free platforms (Shakespeare in Yosemite's work, for example, appears on YouTube).

Finally, eco-Shakespeareans can engage in online conversations: the long line of Shakespearean productions containing ideas that are in themselves recycled allows one to openly draw on antecedents in both form and content. No one is alone in wrestling with the eco-conundrums posed by these plays. That companies have much to celebrate and learn from each other when it comes to eco-Shakespearean practices is a founding principle of the

EarthShakes Alliance, which is a forum for sharing ideas, marking milestones, signposting resources, and creative problem-solving (EarthShakes Alliance, 2024; see also Appendix A). Anyone can join the global online eco-Shakespeare community, becoming part of a continuing, urgent conversation.

Designing *The Tempest* and *Dream: A Conversation*

The following conversation follows on from Katie and Elizabeth's dialogue that ends the previous section. In it, we discuss design, rehearsal, and other practical aspects of the *Tempest* that Elizabeth directed (RSC, 2023) and the *Dream* that Katie directed (Shakespeare in Yosemite, 2024).

Katie: How did you begin conceptualizing the set of your *Tempest*, once you knew that it would focus on a female Prospero and how she and Miranda were surviving on a climate change-impacted island?

Elizabeth: We were very pragmatic about what Prospero and Miranda's world looks like on stage, and what that means for two women on the frontline of climate change. We worked with global climate groups to research how women keep safe in times of catastrophe, everything from how they manage their periods to what Prospero might tell Miranda about how she's growing up, all these basic practicalities of how to eke out a living in a survival situation.

Katie: It also was clear that even though the two of them and Caliban were the only humans around, they were living with the trash and detritus of humanity, with all that junk that's washed up on their shores. I saw ocean trash as a theme, as a fact to learn about, and as an aesthetic. I would love for you to reflect on the difference between aestheticizing ocean trash and showing that it's dangerous.

Elizabeth: With plastic, even if you recycle it, its form is still there. We tried to demonstrate lots of different kinds of interactions with rubbish in the play. That included a human clearing it up; Ferdinand's task was to litter-pick, and he genuinely litter-picked from the audience as well as litter-picking from the stage. We dissolved that line between the audience's reality and the stage reality.

We also had the more-than-human world take rubbish on in terrifying, startling ways. This revealed its ugliness, as when Ariel's harpy wings were made of black bin bags, representing both oil and plastic (see Figure 12).

Figure 12 Heledd Gwynn as Ariel in *The Tempest*, Royal Shakespeare Theatre. Set by Tom Piper. Puppets by Rachael Canning. Photo credit: Ikin Yum

Ariel and the spirits became a huge creature that inhabited the whole stage. A floor-to-ceiling, stage-wide image of ugly plastic confronted the audience and the baddies on stage were asked to reckon with their misdemeanours. Later the dogs were made of large plastic tubs lit with torches [flashlights], and they became very frightening. We revealed the plastic in its full ugliness, and the spirits used it to cleanse the island.

There were other moments where I wanted the rubbish to look beautiful, like the futujara, the flute that Ariel plays (see Figure 13). The instrument is a piece of drainpipe with plastic tubing, inspired by the Recycled Orchestra of Cateura in Paraguay, who make music out of rubbish. We wanted it to be beautiful partly to say: 'there will always be a use for these things. Don't just chuck them away.'

On a pragmatic level, I wanted to draw attention to the way we made the production entirely from reused and recycled materials. There's

Figure 13 Heledd Gwynn as Ariel and Tommy Sim'aan as Caliban in *The Tempest*. Royal Shakespeare Theatre, 2023. Photo credit: Ikin Yum

sometimes a danger at the RSC that audiences assume anything on stage is a beautifully handcrafted prop, that they'd think that someone had painted a crisp packet and put it on stage. I was looking for opportunities to make it clear that this is real rubbish.

Katie: It came through and made me think that trash is central to both ecodramaturgy and eco-practices. I think it's the clearest thing we can use as directors: littering for baddies, litter-picking for characters who are trying to fix things: that's just easy to put on stage. I think we've had a version of it in all our shows.

Elizabeth: You said that for your first *Dream*, that's what people thought it was about.

Katie: Yes, Hippolyta and Theseus in 2018 were littering and they learned not to. And in this recent production, we had Helena picking up trash, some of which had been left by Demetrius. We had a combination of deliberate littering and accidental, because litter is accumulated from both. It is hard to depict oil on stage, but it's easy to depict litter, because it's a human-scaled thing, people can see it. That's why I really love the harpy because it also looked like oil.

Elizabeth: The plastic bottle floating in the sea is an iconic shorthand. And we used that. But we also staged moments like the harpy, when we could make the scaled leap from single human with plastic bottle of water to Big Oil, which has made that plastic bottle. We could make that visible. There was also an oil barrel on the side of the stage, which then became a toy that Miranda played with and rolled around on. It was a cute, innocuous-looking thing, but it's also totally toxic. It was the biggest, most colourful prop on stage: you couldn't ignore it, and it was clearly connected to the rubbish.

Katie: We aestheticized trash as well in our fairy wings, and with the giant sequoia made of recycled boxes. Some of those fairy wings were double recycled because they were 2018 wings that we'd made out of trash that were then made into new fairy wings. We wanted to show how the human world was encroaching upon the animal world and having butterfly wings and bat wings made from trash evoked that. We were also trying to show that we don't need to order fairy wings off Amazon: we have all this stuff we can keep reusing.

Elizabeth: I think the wings were doubly impactful because when I saw them, my first instinct was: 'look at the creativity that's gone into the making of that. It absolutely summons that creature.' And then the longer I looked at them, the more I asked 'why is the embodiment of that tree or that yellow flower fairy made with rubbish?' And I began to see the impact of pollution on those species. Can you tell me more about Snout's Wall, made of snack and cereal boxes?

Katie: I got the idea from Emma Rice's 2016 *Dream*. I was drawn to repeating that technique because with the unpainted, visible boxes, you telegraph that you are using recycled materials (see Figure 14). And a play within the play is a moment to really highlight theatrical

Figure 14 Ranger Marion Roubal as Bottom and Aliyah Hunter as Snout in *A Midsummer Yosemite's Dream*. Yosemite National Park, 2023. Photo Credit: Grace Garnica

eco-practices. In our production the Mechanicals were park rangers, already ecologically minded. Rangers aren't going to go to a craft store to buy poster board to make Wall. They're going to get together and say, 'hey save all your Triscuit and Clif bar boxes for the next few weeks, and that's what we'll use.'

Elizabeth: You reused your own fairy wings in this show, and you said that your ass head for Bottom and a few other props were borrowed from another local company. I found myself loving belonging to this multi-temporal- multi-locational making community and I wonder if you felt something like that too.

Katie: Absolutely. I think that it's best practice ecologically, economically, and socially. It reminds us that we're a community of artists, and we don't need to think of ourselves as in competition with each other, but rather as helping each other. Designers were thrilled to see their work being reused in our *Dream*, and we credited them in the programme to make their work and the practice of borrowing visible. We wanted to plant the idea: if you're doing *Peter Pan*, ask around to see if anyone has a pirate costume before you go buy it on the internet.

Elizabeth: And it helps us position the next bit of the production's life, because it doesn't just end the moment the show ends. I think that's quite a big thought for some theatre makers.

Katie: But community theatres have always done this, have always called the community theatre up the road to ask: 'do you have any costumes we could borrow for *Oliver*!?'

Elizabeth: One of the thought barriers is the idea that there's a unique design that can't be transformed.

Katie: But as with the climate crisis, we have to stop thinking in terms of individual brilliance and instead be thinking about collaboration and cooperation.

Elizabeth: We have to change those narratives, and we have to live those ethics.

Katie: We've talked about how the RSC is both a local company in the middle of Warwickshire and a global brand. When you were working with your design team on this *Tempest*, how did you root it both in this community and also think about global contexts?

Elizabeth: We made the show in partnership with local community organizations. We worked with a group called Rubbish Friends who help keep Stratford clean through volunteer litter picking; all the rubbish in the show came from real rubbish that had been collected from the real Avon and surrounding areas (see Figure 15). We engaged with this local community organization to help in the co-creation of the show and asked the audience to observe what our local environment actually looks like. We also worked with local schools who made sculptures for Miranda and Prospero's shelter and the RSC lobby out of their own recycled materials, and with a local sustainable forestry organization who supplied the organic materials we brought into the world of the play.

Katie: Can you talk more about your rehearsal process? I'd love to hear how design elements arose out of the imaginative play that you facilitate.

78   *Shakespeare Performance*

Figure 15 Litter picking for *The Tempest* in Stratford on Avon. Photo Credit: Ikin Yum

Elizabeth: My rehearsal process is improvisation-based and begins with world-building and relationship-building. Before rehearsals started, the major structural points of the design were in place, all sourced from RSC storage or from previous shows Tom Piper (designer) and I had made. We knew that there would be a broken proscenium arch frame and the forest. But we didn't know what was going to be on the stage, and we didn't know how we were going to do all the things that need to be achieved in the play. We started the rehearsal process with a room full of stuff, some of it from our rubbish collecting partners, some from beach cleans, some from RSC storage or bits that Tom found.

For the first two weeks, the full company would read the text bit by bit, with everybody reading everybody's parts. Together we reached an understanding of the story and began to find the most interesting and playable ways of activating it on stage. Then I would put on some music so that people didn't feel they had to do speaking improvisation. My composer and sound designer Quartly Adrienne made musical choices that affected people's tempo or emotion, and she would be composing on the piano, her computer, or her cello.

The entire company made what we call 'offers' with the bits of set and props and rubbish. And then gradually I asked people who narratively don't need to be in the moment to come out so we end up with, for example, Caliban, Ariel, Miranda, and Prospero in their island world, interacting and making their home. Then, quite quickly, the company created an emotional memory for the characters of 15 years of island life, with what felt like the right set and props to support that backstory. My puppetry director Rachel Canning would watch the company interact with the stuff and figure out what was going to be used to represent a spirit or a dog. My movement director Sarita Piotrowski watched how the company moved around the space. It started to become clear that some things needed to be in the show: that yellow umbrella, that fishing net, that oil barrel. And others didn't.

We did this for every moment and then gradually moved into actual scenes in the play. This meant that the entire company were fully, actively engaged in building every single moment as a collective. Those are how their global, personal lived experiences were then embedded in the entire narrative of the play because that's the choices that those particular humans made.

I steered it and made curatorial decisions, but didn't make impositions. It requires everybody to be present and for us all to hold our nerve. You have to be brave and deal with people wanting you to make decisions by a certain deadline. But it leads to all kinds of imaginative choices you wouldn't otherwise make, and a company who completely inhabit the world of the play. It means the company is comfortable with every element; nothing's a mere prop or costume. They can also improvise their way out of anything during the run of the show!

Katie: This process seems to have so many advantages in terms of empowering your actors and crew, giving them buy-in, and creating a much more interesting world, because it's done by multiple minds.

Elizabeth: I am interested in your approach to design, because you are already performing in an awe-inspiring place. You don't need much in terms of set.

Figure 16 Adam Shulman as Theseus and Sabreena Niles as Hippolyta. Set by Adam Shulman. *A Midsummer Yosemite's Dream*, UC Merced campus, 2024. Photo credit: Amirhadi Shirzadibonab

Katie: It's true. But with this *Dream*, for the first time we had an actual set piece, the base of a giant sequoia at the back of the stage. Sequoias don't grow in the Valley, but you can drive up to a place in the park where they do grow. There are three Sequoia groves in Yosemite, so many spectators could activate their memories of what it's like to be near a sequoia, which is for a lot of us more awe inspiring than even looking at [the peaks] Half Dome or El Capitan.

Our designer built that tree out of my old fence posts and recycled boxes (see Figure 16). It was crucial to the plot, because the tree's fire scar was where the 1930s fairies hid, but also we hoped that it provoked people to think about the majesty of these 3000-year-old trees, and the tragedy of losing 20 per cent of them in the last few years. It was another way to provoke awe. And it is especially important for our campus show, and for what is now the afterlife of all our shows: the YouTube film. In our films, viewers can't see that the stage is surrounded by Half Dome and ponderosa pines, but they can see our cardboard sequoia.

Elizabeth: That's interesting, that when you stage your shows now, you are thinking about an online audience, too.

Katie: Our first responsibility is the in-person audience, but ever since we filmed *Imogen in the Wild* during lockdown in 2021, we've realized that there is a global audience for eco-adapted Shakespeare. And again, because there's no copyright on these plays, we can share them with the world. So every year, we make a film version of our shows that will live on as long as the internet lives on.

Elizabeth: It's also a sustainable way to expand your audience beyond the local.

Katie: I want to ask you about the staging of wonder, too, because in a way that I've never seen before in an indoor performance, your show evoked the wonder of the natural world (see Figure 17).

Figure 17 *The Tempest*, set design by Tom Piper. Royal Shakespeare Theatre, 2023. Photo credit: Ikin Yum

Elizabeth: I wanted to bring the audience to a point of wonder. I really believe in the power of enchantment and that a spell is cast in a theatre. Spectators enter a different imaginative framework and for me the punctuating moment of that process is something that makes one go 'Ahh!'

That's the gift that I can deliver as a theatre maker: moments of awe. But to achieve that inside is tricky. We went right up to the very back wall and opened it out completely. And we didn't use mechanized processes; it was all people, moving stuff, humanly. The show's big reveal at the end was of a green world, evoked by real trees that were coppiced from a nearby woodland. That reveal was an attempt to deliver a moment of natural wonder that reminded the audience of what we're all fighting for, and that there is a better world that we have had, and that we could have again.

There was also real rain. At the end of the play rain fell on Prospero as she did the final epilogue. That's another moment where the real elemental joy of the world was brought inside our auditorium, and it made the space feel expansive and encompassing. Along with the rain, we used a little sapling that Miranda and Ferdinand were given as the goddesses dance and bless their union. They planted it in the upstage forest, and when the show was over, we planted those prop saplings in a real forest.

Katie: It occurs to me that both of our productions really leveraged both the sight of trees and the idea of trees. What do you think it is about trees that helps us think ecologically?

Elizabeth: I wonder if it goes back to what you've said about deep time. We have a sense that many trees were planted long before we were born, and they will exist long after we've died: they evoke deep time. And there is an ancient mythological power in a tree. These are sacred to many cultures around the world; all people know the life-giving potential of a tree. And today we know that they are carbon sinks, and play a major part in saving our future. But they start as a fragile little thing and they need nurture and care and time. They grow slowly and they can't be hurried. I think that if people could find themselves more in tune with the heartbeat of a tree, we might be better fellow citizens of the earth.

Katie: I think there's something about trees that feel hopeful. While Sequoias are thousands of years old, we also know that some trees grow fairly quickly. Humans have intervened so extensively in natural processes that we need to intervene to correct them by planting trees.

Elizabeth: It's something that Shakespeare addresses in his writing. Benvolio talks about the sycamore groves on the western side of Verona (1.1.123). Shakespeare knew that sycamores, because they're fast growing and broad-leaved, are a windbreak. There was so much deforestation already in his time that they planted sycamore groves to get quick shelter, including in Stratford-on-Avon.

The trees, the trash, the visualized forces of nature: there are so many ways Shakespeare allows us to design elements that are crucial to the play's storytelling and its environmental messages, while also broadcasting the sustainable practices involved in the show's creation.

Through this conversation, we hope we have articulated some of our experiences in using green production methods to make Shakespeare shows that can deliver all the moments of action and wonder the texts demand without costing the earth in the process. These are just some of the ways in which we are trying to put our material choices in conversation with our narrative ones. Our practices can be a legible part of our productions, an invitation to both our companies and our audiences to, to paraphrase Lear, take better care of these things.

Epilogue: Green Teaching

'There's woe to come: the children yet unborn shall feel this day as sharp to them as thorn' (*Richard II* 4.1.335–6)

'This is the best and most natural home we are ever going to have. And we need to become a new people to deserve it. We are going to have to be new artists to redream it' (Ben Okri, 2021).

In this Element, we have tried to make the case that Shakespearean plays can be performed and reshaped to convey the urgency and complexity of our planet's environmental problems, and even inspire new alliances and productive, ecological attitude shifts. In addition to being directors and scholars, we are both teachers, too. And we know that when we convey to our students that our own priorities are more focused on the living beings of the twenty-first century than the dead texts of the sixteenth, we are meeting them where they are. We've found that involving students in the creation of ecological Shakespeare projects big and small can be beneficial to their learning and mental health (see also Brokaw, 2023b).

For Shakespeare in Yosemite's *Romeo and Juliet in Yosemite*, our music director and Mercutio, then 25-year-old Tonatiuh Newbold, co-wrote a song that he and Romeo played before the party scene (in this version, they were members of a band, playing the Capulet gig in disguise). The chorus went: 'All I want is to live in a world with you/All I want is the world to exist for you.' Tonatiuh explained that this song is about how for their generation, they aren't sure whether to have kids because of their profound uncertainties about climate change. 'All I want is the world to exist for you': the *you* is the potential child Tona and his fiancée aren't sure they should have. For Generation Z, eco-grief is profound.

We can't solve all our world's immense environmental challenges or easily fix our students' eco-grief, but we have found that two of the things that help our students mitigate their anxieties are collaboration and creativity. And collaboration and creativity are at the heart of engaging with Shakespeare ecologically and adaptively. In fact, researchers have shown that engaging in creative activity helps people process emotions, lower stress, and imagine a more hopeful future (Malaka, 2020).

Such engagement can take many forms, and reach students of all ages through school and university teaching as well as the educational and outreach programming performed by many Shakespeare companies. Students can read eco-criticism and brainstorm how to transform *As You Like It* into a story about their own ecosystem's challenges; share how their own experiences of things like wildfire, heat, or flood help them understand *King Lear* or *The Tempest*; or get involved in a full-scale project like Theo Black's BIOphelia symposium (BIOphelia, 2024). That multi-day event brought together both panels and performative collaborations, including a student-actor Ophelia dispersing plants from Cornell University's botanical garden as a balm for eco-grief (see Figure 18). For companies, this engagement can involve writing and performing ecologically inflected and localized Theatre for Young Audience shows and green shows, or getting younger kids engaged with adaptive Shakespeare through in-school educational

Figure 18 Carolyn Michelle Smith as Gertrude and Oscar Llodra as Laertes in BIOphelia, Cornell University, 2024. Photo credit and production design: Adam Shulman

programming (university students can also get involved with this kind of work). Anything that unleashes young people's best creative and collaborative selves and yokes that energy to a sense of purpose will rehearse the kinds of collective, imaginative creativity Earthlings need to solve local and global ecological challenges.[38]

---

[38] For more on creative, collaborative, embodied, and trauma-informed teaching, see the open-access Camfield, 2025.

Claire Hansen argues that approaching Shakespeare through an ecological, place-based lens can 'enrich our sense of place' and give students a sense that they are connected to something greater than themselves, something that is moving towards meaningful change (2023: 7, 160). At UC Merced, nearly every student who has worked on eco-Shakespeare with Katie has spoken about the project in such terms, explaining that it connected them more fully to where they live while also making them feel a part of a global movement, something that truly matters. These local and global connections, many student collaborators added, were a boon to their mental health: helping them overcome academic, personal, and ecological anxiety; making them feel a sense of community; giving them a sense of purpose.

As the 2020s wear on and mental health issues become an increasingly urgent issue, it becomes ever more imperative that our classrooms and educational programmes inspire confidence, spark creativity, and facilitate connection, rather than – as is too often the case when it comes to Shakespeare – incite feelings of inadequacy. Taking the raw material that is Shakespeare's texts and transforming it to purposeful art is an antidote to pressure-filled, career-focused, profit-motivated education. It meets students literally and figuratively where they are, empowering them to see how their life experiences matter not only to Shakespeare, but to the world.

Appendix A: Selected Eco-Shakespearean Companies and Organizations

The **EarthShakes Alliance**: a global collective of Shakespearean theatres and organizations, each of which pledges to put environmental concerns at the heart of their practices and productions. The website (http://earth shakes.ucmerced.edu) provides several resources including information about the eco-practices of theatres and organizations who are part of the alliance, interviews with eco-theatre makers, annotated bibliographies of ecocriticism, links to eco-Shakespeare resources, and an archive of all of the presentations at the 2021 Globe4Globe: Shakespeare and the Climate Emergency conference. Eco-Shakespearean news is also shared on Instagram: @earthshakesalliance

Bell Shakespeare (Australia) honours the tradition of First Nations touring and accessible storytelling and amplifies relevant geo-political narratives inside the plays.

Butterfly Theatre (UK) specializes in site-responsive Shakespeare in extraordinary locations of natural beauty around the world, like caves and ancient woodlands.

The **Cambridge Shakespeare Festival** (UK) utilizes long, shallow playing spaces to remove the need for amplification and to improve sightlines.

Chesapeake Shakespeare (Maryland, USA) has a touring wagon with built-in lighting and sound systems that are run by solar rechargeable batteries. They are building a second Shakespeare Wagon in 2026 that will be entirely electric.

Come You Spirits (Australia) chooses shows for their themes of natural energy, ancient universal lore, and respect for nature, and edits them to amplify connections to nature.

Flagstaff Shakespeare (Arizona, USA) acknowledges the long presence and stewardship of Indigenous Peoples on the land on which they operate and thus operates a universal lighting and minimal sets and special effects policy.

Gamut Theatre Group (Pennsylvania, USA) has on-site recycling, refillable water stations, and they renovated their building to become more energy efficient.

Gift Horse Theatre (Ireland) champions adapted, ensemble-based work and extends those principles of consideration to the environment. They believe eco-theatre should embrace theatricality, celebrating how it's made rather than trying to hide it.

The **Handlebards** (UK) tour Shakespeare's plays across the UK entirely by bike, with the casts cycling to each new venue carrying the elements of the physical production in panniers.

Island Shakespeare Festival (Washington, USA) reuses materials from season to season and procures from recycling centres and local thrift shops. They create minimal ecological impact in their wooded outdoor space on Whidbey Island.

Montana InSite Theatre uses live, on-site theatre in forests and industrial sites to rework classical texts into immersive experiences that encourage audience members to consider the vital role the nonhuman world plays in their community.

New York City Classical stages shows in public green spaces, which they leave cleaner than they found them. Lighting/radio equipment is rechargeable, and costumes and props are stored locally and re-used.

Oregon Shakespeare Festival has implemented a wildfire policy, with regular monitoring of air quality. They are on the frontlines of elemental eco-theatre, with programming placed alongside human and wildlife health in an urgent and evolving seasonal feedback loop.

Parrabbola (Europe) is a nomadic organization who perform community-based, site-specific works across Europe, including several ecologically themed projects; they also produce the York Shakespeare Festival.

Recycled Shakespeare Company (Maine, USA) asks local businesses for donations of boxes, used bed sheets, and other materials that otherwise would be thrown away, which they use to create sets/props/costumes. Post show, all materials are saved or recycled (see Section 3).

The **Royal Shakespeare Company** (UK) now makes its productions in line with Theatre Green Book standards. Off-stage, the company is in the

Appendix A: Selected Eco-Shakespearean Companies

process of moving all its lighting to LED and running its estate on 100 per cent green electricity.

The Rude Mechanicals (UK) tour across the south east of England scheduling tours to maximise travel efficiency and minimise emissions.

Santa Cruz Shakespeare (California, USA) is a registered green business, and have a volunteer team of stewards who maintain the land on which their amphitheatre is built.

Shakespeare in the Arb (Michigan, USA) is a collaboration between Matthaei Botanical Gardens, Nichols Arboretum, and the University of Michigan Residential College. The audience moves with the actors as the play unfolds throughout the 120-acre Nichols Arboretum.

Shakespeare Birthplace Trust (UK) have made their sites greener, including transferring energy contracts to renewable suppliers for both gas and electricity and removing single use plastic bottles from retail. They have worked with local beekeepers and hedgehog rescue projects and aim to be carbon neutral by 2030.

Shakespeare's Globe (UK) often performs with no lights or sound equipment, and has done ecological audits of several productions. They hosted the Globe4Globe: Shakespeare and the Climate Emergency conference in 2021, which will return in fall 2025.

Shakespeare in Paradise (Bahamas) has done several ecologically themed productions, often highlighting the islands' vulnerability to hurricanes.

Shakespeare South (Australia) explores how ecological performance can be beautiful, engaging and uplifting. They use green theatre tools and dynamic staging in living environments or use biophilic scenography in indoor spaces.

Shakespeare in the Woods (Vermont, USA) reuses, reworks, and upcycles costumes and props and draws from their natural outdoor space for much of their scene design.

Shakespeare in Yosemite (California, USA) performs heavily adapted, ecologically themed productions of Shakespeare every Earth Day weekend, in the Curry Village amphitheatre in Yosemite National Park.

Theatricum Botanicum (California, USA) is an open-air performance site and botanical garden, with living examples of many of the plants mentioned in John Parkinson's seventeenth-century plant encyclopaedia. They engage with local river clean-ups and other community-focused ecological activities.

The Stratford Festival (Ontario, Canada) pays respect to the ancestral guardians of the land and waterways on which it operates and encourages a practice of shared and reciprocal resource use across its productions.

The Willow Globe (Y Glôb Byw) (Wales) is a scaled-down version of Shakespeare's Globe, made from living willow, sculpted into an organic structure. It is on a working farm, with an alternative wet-weather venue in the form of a big-top circus tent (see O'Malley, 2018).

For an updated list and more information, visit these company's websites, or http://earthshakes.ucmerced.edu.

Appendix B: Selected Eco-Shakespearean Productions and Films

All's Well That Ends Well

- OrangeMite Theatre (Pennsylvania, USA), 2022: set the play at summer camp, where campers learned from an enthusiastic park ranger who shared *The Ornithology of Shakespeare* throughout the play. The young protagonists discovered how to strengthen relationships with one another and the natural world.

As You Like It

- Regent's Park Open Air Theatre (UK), 2018: contrasted a corporate court with an Arden where exiles turned oil drums into planters and worked to green their environment
- Shakespeare in Yosemite, 2019: hung scientific information about the Sierra Nevada forest, wildfire, and climate adaptation to trees near the venue along with Orlando's poems, and the final dance was a climate march (see Brokaw 2021 and 2023a)
- Watermill (UK), 2021: a court filled with oil drums and construction detritus contrasted the lush forest surrounding the site, which doubled as Arden. During an epilogue on climate and sustainability, actors brought on placards with environmental messages before singing 'Set My Soul on Fire'.

Coriolanus

- Shakespeare in the Woods (Vermont, USA), 2022: asked, 'How do we put an end to man's insatiable hunger – for sustenance, resources, power? Is overconsumption a man's problem?' and was staged through the lens of asylum-seeking refugees in a present-day immigration centre. It made clear connections between food insecurity and eco-crises.

Cymbeline

All of the following productions were part of the *Cymbeline in the Anthropocene* project, which brought together theatres from around the world to stage or film ecologically adapted *Cymbeline*s in 2021, and hosted a symposium in 2022 www.cymbeline-anthropocene.com/. Most productions and films can be viewed at www.youtube.com/@cymbeline-anthropocene6847.

- Cornell University Theatre Department (New York, USA): video adaptation titled *Once Upon a Time in the Anthropocene*
- Exeter University (UK): two short adaptations, *Gold and Silver Turned to Dust* explored corporate land grabs, and *Does the World Go Round*, on human greed
- LaTrobe University (Australia): transformed the play's war into a bushfire
- Montana Shakespeare in the Park: performed against a backdrop of mountains and wildfires across Montana, in an ecologically conscious touring production (see Minton and Gray, 2022)
- Setebos Theatre Company (Argentina): retitled *Cimbelino en la Patagonia* and adapted to draw on Indigenous South American mythology (see Section 1)
- Shakespeare in Yosemite: retitled *Imogen in the Wild* and filmed on location in Yosemite to highlight links between land abuse and misogyny (see Brokaw, 2023b)
- Willow Globe (Wales): set in their open-air replica of the Globe made out of willow (see discussion earlier and Section 3)

Hamlet

- National Theatre Beaivváš (Sweden), 2003: produced in a replica of the Globe made out of ice, and translated into the Indigenous Sámi language, and called attention to the way diminishing ice and snow affects those communities (see Duckert, 2025).

Appendix B: Selected Eco-Shakespearean Productions and Films

King Lear

- LaTrobe Theatre (Australia), 2017: an outdoor promenade student production that highlighted the importance of trees and ecological reciprocity (see Conkie, 2018).
- For more on ecocritical *Lear* in production, see Hamilton, 2017.

Love's Labor's Lost

- Michigan State University, 2008: a documented green production, staged as a case study for creating greener theatre (see Miller, 2012).
- Shakespeare in Yosemite, 2022: set in 1969 and 1970 and commemorating the youth-led environmental movements that lead to the first Earth Day and American environmental legislation, with the opposing groups as bands on songwriting retreat in Yosemite (see Brokaw, 2023a).

Macbeth

- Joburg Theatre Youth Development Programme (South Africa), 2022: replaced some dialogue with bird song and performed in several South African languages and vernaculars, indigenizing and decolonizing the text (see Section 2).
- Montana Shakespeare in the Parks, 2017: highlighted the importance of public lands and was set in a post-apocalyptic period following a global collapse brought on by climate change. It sought to draw links between tyranny in kingdoms and ecosystems (see Minton, 2018).
- National Theatre of Great Britain, 2018: set in a near-future apocalypse, the set was partially composed of black garbage bags, and the play's violence was clearly tied to a need to scavenge for scarce resources.

Merry Wives of Windsor

- Recycled Shakespeare Company (USA), 2023: production featured ecological elements throughout, including having Falstaff carried out in a recycling bin.

A Midsummer Night's Dream

- Burgtheatre (Austria), 2020: explored the play in the context of climate catastrophes and patriarchal systems that deny fluidity in all its forms.
- Butterfly Theatre (UK), 2022: staged in two different caverns in the UK, highlighting the play's darkness and the ecosystems of caves.
- Nashville Shakespeare Festival (USA), 2014: featured fairy costumes made of 100 per cent recycled materials. An on-site seed bomb station encouraged audience members to create seed bombs to beautify forgotten places around the city and photograph the flowers after they bloomed.
- Rough Magic (Ireland), 2018: set in a semi-apocalyptic future and exploring the recklessness of mankind in the face of a misunderstood ecosystem (see Daroy and Prescott, 2025: 144–6).
- San Francisco Shakespeare Festival, 2022: touring production that highlighted ecological themes, and indigenized the fairy costumes with California flora and fauna.
- Shakespeare in Yosemite, 2018: highlighted issues of overconsumption and its effect on the natural world (see Brokaw and Prescott, 2022).
- Shakespeare in Yosemite, 2024: see Sections 2 and 3.

Pericles

- Shakespeare in Napa, 2016: explored global issues of sex trafficking, the media, and the effects of global warming.

Appendix B: Selected Eco-Shakespearean Productions and Films 95

Romeo and Juliet

- Shakespeare in Yosemite, 2023: transplanted the action to Yosemite, featuring forest fires, floods, and the true story of the successful reintroduction of red-legged frogs to the Sierra mountain ecosystem

The Tempest

- Illinois Shakespeare Festival, 2023: theatre for young audience show *Toss Me a Tempest* adapted the play to be about Caliban and Ariel teaching Prospero how to live in balance, and converting the island into a nature camp for children at the end of the show.
- Montana InSite Theatre, 2020: a short film called *A Nigerian Eco-Tempest: Oguta Island* explored the human and environmental damages of colonialism, and reimagined Caliban as a figure with full knowledge of African history who embodied resistance to colonialism.
- Royal Shakespeare Company, 2023: see Sections 2 and 3.
- Shakespeare in Paradise, 2009 (Bahamas): turned Prospero into a former CEO, which spoke to Bahamians' colonial past and environmental present.
- Shakespeare in the Woods (Vermont), 2023: focused on dynamics between Prospero and Caliban and Ariel, recognizing the act of land seizure that has occurred and its effect on the ecosystem while encouraging audiences to think about the colonial history of New England.

Timon of Athens

- Montana InSite Theatre, 2019: in the adaptation *Timon of Anaconda*, the action of the play is moved to the mining town Butte, which is now one of the USA's largest superfund sites (see Minton, 2021).

Twelfth Night

- Royal Shakespeare Company, 2022: touring production for young people featured recycled design elements.
- Shakespeare South (Australia), 2022: performed in a botanic garden and encouraging 'biophelia' in its audiences, and carbon offset with biodiversity restoration programmes.

Multi-Work Projects

- Parrabbola (Europe), 2020: *This Distemperature*, a five-act audio juxtaposition of extracts from Shakespeare's plays and poems with Greenpeace articles, news footage, Greta Thunberg speeches, and more.
- Shakespeare's Globe (UK), 2021: *Letters to the Earth*, a nearly 6 minute-YouTube video excerpting various lines of Shakespeare and juxtaposing them with footage of climate disasters, with an introduction setting up Shakespeare's ecological relevance.
- University of Cornell (USA), 2024: *BIOphelia*, a multidisciplinary symposium exploring an eco-feminist revival of the shared roles between Ophelia and her plants, featuring student-centred practice-based-research, performance workshops, and scholar-led discussions.

Appendix C: Selected Eco-Theatre and Eco-Arts Organizations and Resources

Artists & Climate Change: https://artistsandclimatechange.com/
Artivist Network: www.artivistnetwork.org/
Broadway Green Alliance (BGA): www.broadwaygreen.com
Centre for Sustainable Practice in the Arts: www.sustainablepractice.org/
Climate Change Theatre Action: www.climatechangetheatreaction.com/
Culture Declares: www.culturedeclares.org/
Ecostage: https://ecostage.online/
Groundwater Arts: www.groundwaterarts.com/
HowlRound Theatre: https://howlround.com/climate-change-eco-theatre
Julie's Bicycle: https://juliesbicycle.com
Resilient Revolt: https://resilientrevolt.org/
Theatre Green Book: https://theatregreenbook.com/
Theatre Without Borders: https://theatrewithoutborders.com/

References

All quotations from Shakespeare come from the Folger Shakespeare Library editions, Barbara Mowat and Paul Werstine, eds.

Works preceded by an * are available for free online.

*About EMSOC (2025). www.emsoc.co.uk/about

*Allen, Summer (2018) *The Science of Awe*. A white paper prepared for the John Templeton Foundation by the Greater Good Science Center at UC Berkeley. https://ggsc.berkeley.edu/images/uploads/GGSC-JTF_White_Paper-Awe_FINAL.pdf.

*Almeida, Paul, Luis Rubén González, Edward Orozco Flores, Venise Curry and Ana Padilla (2023) 'The Building Blocks of Community Participation in Local Climate Meetings. *Npj Climate Action* 2: 1–5. https://doi.org/10.1038/s44168-023-00071-4.

Allred, Gemma Kate, Benjamin Broadribb and Erin Sullivan (eds.) (2022) *Lockdown Shakespeare: New Evolutions in Performance and Adaptation*. London: Bloomsbury.

Angelaki, Vicky (2019) *Theatre and Environment*. London: Bloomsbury.

Arnold, Annika (2018) *Climate Change and Storytelling Narratives and Cultural Meaning in Environmental Communication*. London: Palgrave.

Arons, Wendy and Theresa J. May (eds.) (2012) *Readings in Performance and Ecology*. London: Palgrave.

Beer, Tanja (2021) *Ecoscenography: An Introduction to Ecological Design for Performance*. London: Palgrave.

Berners-Lee, Mike (2020) *How Bad Are Bananas?: The Carbon Footprint of Everything*. London: Profile Books.

Bilodeau, Chantal (2020) 'Introduction' in Chantal Bilodeau and Thomas Peterson (eds.), *Lighting the Way: An Anthology of Short Plays about the Climate Crisis*. Toronto: Centre for Sustainable Practice in the Arts, 15–23.

*BIOphelia: A Performance-Infused Scholarship Symposium (2024) 16–19 October. https://pma.cornell.edu/news/biophelia-performance-infused-scholarship-symposium.

*Borderlands Shakespeare Collectiva (2024) https://borderlandsshakespeare.org/.

*Borlik, Todd (2024) 'Shakespeare and the Environment', Shakespeare Unlimited Podcast. www.folger.edu/podcasts/shakespeare-unlimited/shakespeare-environment-borlik/.

(2023) *Shakespeare beyond the Green World: Drama and Ecopolitics in Jacobean Britain*. Oxford: Oxford University Press.

Boykoff, Maxwell (2019) *Creative (Climate) Communications: Productive Pathways for Science, Policy, and Society*. Cambridge: Cambridge University Press.

Bradley, Kath (2024) 'Performance Review: *The Tempest* by Elizabeth Freestone', *Cahiers Élisabéthains* 113(1): 105–108.

Braungart, Michael and McDonough, William (2002) *Cradle to Cradle, Remaking the Way We Make Things*. London: Vintage.

Brokaw, Katherine Steele (2021) 'Text-Based / Concept-Driven,' in Claire Bourne (ed.), *Shakespeare/Text: Arden Critical Intersections*. London: Arden Bloomsbury.

(2023a) *Shakespeare and Community Performance*. London: Palgrave.

(2023b) 'Shakespeare and Environmental Justice: Collaborative Eco-Theatre in Yosemite National Park and the San Joaquin Valley', in Marissa Greenberg and Elizabeth Williamson (eds.), *Situating Shakespeare in Higher Education: Social Justice and Institutional Contexts*. Edinburgh: Edinburgh University Press, 94–110.

*Brokaw, Katherine Steele and Abrian Curington (2024) 'Shakespeare as Environmental Writer'. *UC Merced: Center for the Humanities Bobcat Comics*. https://escholarship.org/uc/item/2c67c46t.

Brokaw, Katherine Steele and Paul Prescott (2022) 'Reduce, Rewrite, Recycle: Adapting Shakespeare for the Environment', in Diana Henderson and Stephen O'Neill (eds.), *The Arden Research Companion to Shakespeare and Adaptation*, London: Bloomsbury, 303–322.

Brown, Adrienne Maree (2017) *Emergent Strategy*. Chico, CA: AK Press.

——— (2023) 'Imagination is a Muscle', in Rebecca Solnit, Thelma Young, and Lutunata Bua (eds.), *Not Too Late: Changing the Climate Story from Despair to Possibility*, Chicago: Haymarket Books, 151–157.

Bruckner, Lynne (2011) 'Teaching Shakespeare in the Ecotone', in Lynne Bruckner and Dan Brayton (eds.), *Ecocritical Shakespeare*. Aldershot: Ashgate, 151–157.

Buell, Lawrence (2005) *The Future of Environmental Criticism: Environmental Crisis and Literary Imagination*. Oxford: Blackwell.

*Butfield, Colin (2020) 'Storytellers Can Help Save the Planet'. *World Economic Forum*, www.weforum.org/agenda/2020/09/storytellers-open-planet-data-footage-wwf/.

Butler, Octavia (1993) *Parable of the Sower*. New York: Grand Central.

——— (1998) *Parable of the Talents*. New York: Grand Central Publishing.

*Camfield, Eileen (ed.) (2025) *Joy-Centered Pedagogy in Higher Education: Uplifting Teaching and Learning for All*. London: Routledge.

Carlson, Marvin (2003) *The Haunted Stage: The Theatre as Memory Machine*. Michigan: University of Michigan Press.

Carroll, Sean B. (2009) *The Making of the Fittest: DNA and the Ultimate Forensic Record of Evolution*. London: Quercus.

Chattoo, Caty Borum and Lauren Feldman and Norman Lear (2020) *A Comedian and an Activist Walk into a Bar: The Serious Role of Comedy in Social Justice*. Berkeley: University of California Press.

Chaudhuri, Una (1994) '"There Must Be a Lot of Fish in That Lake": Toward an Ecological Theatre', *Theatre* 25(1): 23–31.

Chaudhuri, Una and Joshua Williams (2020) 'The Play at the End of the World: Deke Weaver's *Unreliable Bestiary* and the Theatre of Extinction', in Kristen E. Shepherd-Barr (eds.), *Cambridge Companion to Theatre and Science*. Cambridge: Cambridge University Press, 70–84.

Childress, Jennifer, Backman, Alysia Cella, and Lipson, Marjorie Y. (2020–1) 'Reframing Literacy Assessment: Using Scales and Micro-Progressions to Provide Equitable Assessments for All Learners', *Journal of Adolescent & Adult Literacy* 63(4): 371–377.

Clark, Timothy (2014) 'Nature, Post-Nature', in Louise Westling (ed.), *Cambridge Companion to Literature and the Environment*. Cambridge: Cambridge University Press, 75–89.

Cless, Dominic (2012) 'Ecodirecting Canonical Plays', in Wendy Arons and Theresa May (eds.), *Readings in Performance and Ecology*. New York: Palgrave Macmillan, 159–168.

Conkie, Rob (2018) 'Nature's Above Art', *Shakespeare Bulletin* 36 (3): 391–408.

Cook, Simon, Stevenson, Lorna, Aldred, Rachel, Kendall, Matt and Tom Cohen (2022) 'More than Walking and Cycling: What Is "Active Travel"?' *Transport Policy* 126: 151–161.

Corredera, Vanessa I., L. Monique Pittman and Geoffrey Way (eds.) (2023) *Shakespeare and Cultural Appropriation*. London: Routledge.

Crutzen, Paul J. and Stoermer, Eugene F. (2000) 'The Anthropocene', *IGBP Global Change News* 41, 17–18.

Cymbeline in the Anthropocene (2022) cymbeline-anthropocene.com.

Damasio, Antonio (2022) *Feeling and Knowing: Making Minds Conscious*. New York: Vintage.

Daroy, Alys (2022) 'Biophilic Shakespeare: Towards and Ecology of Form', PhD Thesis, University of Warwick.

(2020) 'Shakespeare and Climate Change', Shakespeare's Globe Blog. 22 April. www.shakespearesglobe.com/discover/blogs-and-features/2020/04/22/shakespeare-and-climate-change/.

Daroy, Alys and Paul Prescott (2025) *Shakespeare, Ecology, and Adaptation*. London: Arden Bloomsbury.

Day, Timothy Ryan (2021) *Shakespeare and the Evolution of the Human Umwelt: Adapt, Interpret, Mutate*. London: Routledge.

Denton, F., T. J. Wilbanks, A. C. Abeysinghe, et al. (2014) 'Climate-Resilient Pathways: Adaptation, Mitigation, and Sustainable Development', in *Climate Change 2014: Impacts, Adaptation, and Vulnerability*. Cambridge: Cambridge University Press, 1101–1131.

Dionne, Craig (2020) 'Cognitive Ethology Studies', in Evelyn Gajowski (ed.), *The Arden Research Handbook of Contemporary Shakespeare Criticism*. London: Bloomsbury, 305–319.

Duckert, Lowell (2025) *Cold Doings: Early Modern Actions for our Warmer World*. Minneapolis: University of Minnesota Press.

Duncan, Sophie (2019) *Shakespeare's Props: Memory and Cognition*. London: Routledge.

EarthShakes Alliance (2024) http://earthshakes.ucmerced.edu.

Egan, Gabriel (2006) *Green Shakespeare: From Ecopolitics to Ecocriticism*. London: Palgrave.

End Climate Science (2025) www.endclimatesilence.org.

Espinosa, Ruben (2021) *Shakespeare on the Shades of Racism*. London: Routledge.

Estok, Simon (2011) *Ecocriticism and Shakespeare: Reading Ecophobia*. London: Palgrave.

Evans, Mel (2015) *Artwash: Big Oil and the Arts*. London: Pluto Press.

Fagan, Brian (2001) *The Little Ice Age: How Climate Made History 1300–1850*. New York: Basic.

Fairlie, Simon (2009) 'A Short History of Enclosure in Britain', *The Land* 7: 16–31.

Fanelli, Carlo (2016) 'Vision and Imagination in the Renaissance Theatre', *Journal of Literature and Art Studies* 6(2): 146–165.

Fischer-Lichte, Ericka (2008) *The Transformative Power of Performance*. London: Routledge.

Fournier, Emily (2020) Interview with Ying-Wei Zhang. EarthShakes Website. https://earthshakes.ucmerced.edu/resources/interviews-theatre-makers.

Freestone, Elizabeth (2024) 'A Midsummer Yosemite's Dream,' *Shakespeare Bulletin* 42(3): 418–422.

Freestone, Elizabeth and Jeanie O'Hare (2021) *100 Plays to Save the World*. London: Nick Hern Books.

Frye, Northrop (1957) *Anatomy of Criticism*. Princeton: Princeton University Press.

Garrett, Ian (2012) 'Theatrical Production's Carbon Footprint', in Wendy Arons and Theresa May (eds.), *Readings in Performance and Ecology*. New York: Palgrave Macmillan, 201–210.

Gerard, John (1597) *Herball, or General Historie of Plantes*. London: John Norton.

*Gharib, Malaka (2020) 'Feeling Artsy: Here's How Making Art Helps Your Brain', National Public Radio. 11 January. www.npr.org/sections/health-shots/2020/01/11/795010044/feeling-artsy-heres-how-making-art-helps-your-brain.

Ghosh, Amitav (2016) *The Great Derangement: Climate Change and the Unthinkable*. Chicago: University of Chicago Press.

Gifford, Terry (2014) 'Pastoral, Anti-Pastoral, and Post-Pastoral', in Louise Westling (ed.), *Cambridge Companion to Literature and the Environment*. Cambridge: Cambridge University Press, 17–30.

Goldfinger, Jacqueline and Allison Horsely (2023) *Writing Adaptations and Translations for the Stage: A Guide and Workbooks for New and Experienced Writers*. London: Routledge.

Graeber, David (2015) *The Utopia of Rules*. New York: Melville House.

Gray, Hugh and Terrence Hawkes (2007) *Presentist Shakespeares*. London: Routledge.

Green Digital Action (2025) www.itu.int/initiatives/green-digital-action/.

Green, William David (2023) 'Review of William Shakespeare's *The Tempest*', *Shakespeare* 19(4): 592–595.

Greenwood, Emily (2016) 'Reception Studies: The Cultural Mobility of Classics', *Daedalus* 145(2), 41–49.

Guenther, Genevieve (2024) *The Language of Climate Politics: Fossil-Fuel Propaganda and How to Fight It*. Oxford: Oxford University Press.

Hamilton, Jennifer Mae (2017) *This Contentious Storm: An Ecocritical and Performance History of King Lear*. London: Bloomsbury.

Harraway, Donna (2016) *Staying with the Trouble*. Durham: Duke University Press.

Hawkes, Terence and Hugh Grady (eds.) (2007) *Presentist Shakespeares*. London: Routledge.

Henderson, Diana (2006) *Collaborations with the Past: Reshaping Shakespeare across Time and Media*. Ithaca: Cornell University Press.

Henderson, Diana and Stephen O'Neill (eds.) (2022) *The Arden Research Handbook of Shakespeare and Adaptation*. London: Bloomsbury.

Horvath, Christina and Juliet Carpenter (eds.) (2020) *Co-Creation in Theory and Practice: Exploring Creativity in the Global North and Global South*. Bristol: Policy Press.

Hoydis, Julia, Roman Bartosch, and Jens Martin Gurr (2023) *Climate Change Literacy*. Cambridge: Cambridge University Press.

*ICAO Carbon Emissions Calculator (2025) www.icao.int/environmental-protection/CarbonOffset/Pages/default.aspx.

*International Commission on Stratigraphy (2024) https://stratigraphy.org/.

Kallenbach, Ulla (2018) *The Theatre of Imagining: A Cultural History of Imagination in the Mind and on the Stage*. New York: Springer Nature.

Karim-Cooper, Farah, and Stern, Tiffany (eds.) (2013) *Shakespeare's Theatres and the Effects of Performance*. London: Bloomsbury.

Kidnie, Margaret Jane (2009) *Shakespeare and the Problem of Adaptation*. London: Routledge.

*Kimmerer, Robin Wall (2022) 'Ancient Green: Moss, Climate, and Deep Time', *Emergence Magazine*. 20 April. https://emergencemagazine.org/essay/ancient-green/.

Kolbert, Elizabeth (2016) *The Sixth Extinction: An Unnatural History*. New York: Picador.

Kulick, Brian (2023) *Staging the End of the World: Theatre in a Time of Climate Crisis*. London: Methuen Drama.

Laroche, Rebecca and Jennifer Munroe (2017) *Shakespeare and Ecofeminism*. London: Arden Bloomsbury.

Lawson, Mark (2023) '*The Tempest* Review—Alex Kingston is a Magnificent Prospero', *The Guardian*, 3 February. www.theguardian.com/stage/2023/feb/03/the-tempest-review-alex-kingston-prospero-royal-shakespeare-stratford.

Leitch, Thomas (ed.) (2017) *The Oxford Handbook of Adaptation Studies*. Oxford: Oxford Academic.

Lewis, Simon and Maslin, Mark (2015) 'Defining the Anthropocene', *Nature* 519: 171–180.

Love, Catherine (2020) 'From Facts to Feelings: The Development of Katie Mitchell's Ecodramaturgy', *Contemporary Theatre Review* 30(2): 226–235.

(2021) Eco-theatre and the Anthropocene: Katie Mitchell in Conversation. TORCH. The Oxford Research Centre in the Humanities.

Linthicum, Kent (2022) 'Energy and the Anthropocene', in Seth Reno (ed.), *The Anthropocene: Approaches and Contexts for Literature and the Humanities*. London: Routledge, 38–49.

Lipson, E. (1931) *Economic History of England*. London: A&C Black.

MacFaul, Tom (2015) *Shakespeare and the Natural World*. Cambridge: Cambridge University Press.

Macmillan, Duncan (2011) *Lungs*. London: Oberton Books Ltd.

*Macrine, Sheila and Jennifer Fugate (eds.) (2022) *Movement Matters: How Embodied Cognition Informs Teaching and Learning*. Cambridge, MA: MIT Press. https://doi.org/10.7551/mitpress/13593.001.0001.

Mann, Michael E (2022) *The New Climate War: The Fight to Take Back Our Planet*. New York: PublicAffairs.

Martin, Randall (2015) *Shakespeare and Ecology*. Oxford: Oxford University Press.

(2017) 'Shakespeare, Ecology, and the Environment'. Folger Library Blog. 18 April. www.folger.edu/blogs/shakespeare-and-beyond/shakespeare-ecology-environmental-earth-day/.

Martin, Randall and Evelyn O'Malley (2018) 'Eco-Shakespeare in Performance: Introduction', *Shakespeare Bulletin* 36(3): 377–390.

May, Theresa J. (2021) *Earth Matters on Stage: Ecology and Environment in the American Theatre*. London: Routledge.

(2022) 'Kinship and Community in Climate-Change Theatre: Ecodramaturgy in Practice', *Journal of Contemporary Drama in English* 10(1): 164–182.

(2010) 'Kneading Marie Clements' *Burning Vision*', *Canadian Theatre Review* 144: 5–12.

(2005) 'Greening the Theatre: Taking Ecocriticism from Page to Stage', *Interdisciplinary Literary Studies* 7(1): 84–103.

McConachie, Bruce (2012) 'Ethics, Evolution, Ecology, and Performance', in Wendy Arons and Theresa J. May (eds.), *Readings in Performance and Ecology*. London: Palgrave Macmillan, 91–100.

McKibben, Bill (1989) *The End of Nature*. London: Random House.

(2005) 'What the Warming World Needs Now is Art, Sweet Art'. *Grist*, https://grist.org/article/mckibben-imagine/.

*McNulty, Charles (2025) 'Shakespeare's "The Tempest" Illuminates an Existential Truth Revealed by the Los Angeles Fires'. *Los Angeles Times*. 13 January. www.latimes.com/entertainment-arts/story/2025-01-13/los-angeles-fires-shakespeare-tempest.

Midsummer Yosemite's Dream (2024) Shakespeare in Yosemite Website. https://yosemiteshakes.ucmerced.edu/spring-2024-dream.

Milkoreit, Manjana (2016) 'The Promise of Climate Fiction: Imagination, Storytelling, and the Politics of the Future', in Paul Wapner and Hilal Elver (eds.), *Reimagining Climate Change*. London: Routledge, 171–191.

Miller, Justin A. (2012) 'The Labor of Greening *Love's Labour's Lost*', in Wendy Arons and Theresa J. May (eds.), *Readings in Performance and Ecology*. London: Palgrave Macmillan, 201–210.

*Mingins, Phillippa (2023) 'RSC's *The Tempest* Leads to Soar in Litter Picking Interest'. *The Stratford Observer*. 22 February. https://stratfordobserver.co.uk/news/rscs-the-tempest-leads-to-soar-in-litter-picking-interest/.

*Minton, Gretchen (2021) 'Ecological Adaptation in Montana: *Timon of Athens* to *Timon of Anaconda*', *New Theatre Quarterly* 37(1): 20–37. www.cambridge.org/core/blog/2021/03/04/mining-shakespeare/.

Minton, Gretchen and Mikey Gray (2022) 'The Ecological Journey of Imogen in Montana's Parks', *New Theatre Quarterly* 38(4): 299–318.

(2018) '"The Season of All Natures": Montana Shakespeare in the Park's Global Warming *Macbeth*'. *Shakespeare Bulletin* 36(3): 428–448.

*MIT Global Shakespeare Project (2024) https://shakespeareproject.mit.edu/.

*Moezzi, Mithra, Kathryn B. Janda and SeaRotmann (2017) 'Using Stories, Narratives, and Storytelling in Energy and Climate Change Research', *Energy Research and Social Science* 31(1): 1–10, https://doi.org/10.1016/j.erss.2017.06.034.

Munroe, Jennifer (2016) 'It's All About the Gillyvors: Engendering Art and Nature in *The Winter's Tale*,' in Lynne Bruckner and Dan Brayton (eds.), *Ecocritical Shakespeare*. London: Routledge, 139–154.

Nardizzi, Vincent Joseph (2013) *Wooden Os*. Toronto: Toronto University Press.

Nicholson, Helen (2014) *Applied Drama: The Gift of the Theatre*. Basingstoke: Palgrave Macmillan.

Oakley-Brown, Liz (2024) *Shakespeare on the Ecological Surface*. Oxford: Routledge, Spotlight on Shakespeare.

*'Octavia Butler Imagined LA Ravished by Fires' (2025) *US News and World Report*. 14 January. www.usnews.com/news/best-states/california/articles/2025-01-14/octavia-butler-imagined-la-ravaged-by-fires-her-altadena-cemetery-survived.

O'Dair, Sharon (2011) 'Is it Shakespearean Ecocriticism if it isn't Presentist?', in Lyn Bruckner and Dan Brayton (eds.), *Ecocritical Shakespeare*. Aldershot: Ashgate, 71–85.

*Okri, Ben (2021) Artists must confront the climate crisis. *The Guardian*. 12 November. www.theguardian.com/commentisfree/2021/nov/12/artists-climate-crisis-write-creativity-imagination.

O'Malley, Evelyn (2018) '"To Weather a Play": Audiences, Outdoor Shakespeares, and Avant-Garde Nostalgia at the Willow Globe', *Shakespeare Bulletin* 36(3): 409–427.

(2020) *Weathering Shakespeare: Audiences and Open-Air Performance*. London: Bloomsbury.

O'Shea, Meg (2011) 'Arts Engagement with Sustainable Communities: Informing New Governance Styles', *Sustainable Futures, Culture and Local Governance* 3(1–2): 29–41.

Ottum, Lisa (2022) 'The Deep Time Life Kit: Thinking Tools for the Anthropocene', in Seth Reno (ed.), *The Anthropocene: Approaches and Contexts for Literature and the Humanities*. London: Routledge, 13–25.

Parkinson, John (1640) *Theatrum Botanicum: The Theatre of Plantes*. London: Tho. Cotes.

Pearce, Warren, Reinger Grundmann, Mike Hulme et al. (2017) 'Beyond Counting Climate Consensus', *Environmental Communication* 11(6): 723–730.

Pedelty, Mark (2012) *Ecomusicology: Rock, Folk and the Environment*. Philadelphia, PA: Temple University Press.

Perkins Wilder, L. (2010). *Shakespeare's Memory Theatre: Recollection, Properties, and Character*. Cambridge: Cambridge University Press.

Pollock, Sheldon, Benjamin Elman, and Ku-ming Kevin Chang (eds.) (2015) *World Philology*. Cambridge, MA: Perkins Wilder.

*Raceb4Race (2025) www.emsoc.co.uk/about.

Rathje, Steve, Leor Hackel and Jamil Zaki (2021) 'Attending Live Theatre Improves Empathy, Changes Attitudes, and Leads to Pro-social Behavior', *Journal of Experimental Social Psychology* 95. https://doi.org/10.1016/j.jesp.2021.104138.

Reno, Seth T. (2022) 'Introduction: The Anthropocene and the Humanities', in Seth Reno (ed.), *The Anthropocene: Approaches and Contexts for Literature and the Humanities*. London: Routledge, 1–10.

*Rich, Nathaniel (2024) 'Climate Change is Making us Paranoid, Anxious, and Angry', *The New York Times*, 9 April. www.nytimes.com/2024/

04/09/books/review/the-weight-of-nature-clayton-page-aldern.html.

Ridout, Nicholas (2009) *Theatre & Ethics*. London: Palgrave Macmillan.

Rivas, Jessica (2018) Interview with Katie Brokaw, 22 April.

Roberts, Sarah (2022) 'Sounding the Polyphonic Cacophony of Macbeth with a Young Jozi Ensemble', *Shakespeare in Southern Africa* 35: 4–18.

RSC *Tempest* (2023) Website. www.rsc.org.uk/the-tempest/past-productions/elizabeth-freestone-2023-production.

Rueckert, William (1978, 1996) 'Literature and Ecology: An Experiment in Ecocriticism', in Cheryll Glotfelty and Harold Fromm (eds.), *The Ecocriticism Reader: Landmarks in Literary Ecology*. Edited by Athens, GA: University of Georgia Press, 105–123. Originally published in 1978.

Ruiter, David, ed. (2021) *The Arden Research Handbook of Shakespeare and Social Justice*. London: Arden Bloomsbury.

Saenger, Michael (2016) '"Do not call them Bastards": Shakespeare as an Invasive Species', *Palgrave Communications* (2): 1–6, https://doi.org/10.1057/palcomms.2016.65.

Sanders, Julie (2023) 'Lines of Control and Global Social Justice: Shakespearean Adaptation, British Colonial and Contemporary India and the Question of Kashmir', In Brandon Chua, and Elizabeth Ho (eds.), *The Routledge Companion to Global Literary Adaptation in the Twenty-First Century* (1st ed.) Routledge.

Sayet, Madeline (2021) 'Where Does the Story Meet the Earth?' Globe4Globe Conference Presentation. 22 April. Online.

*Shakespeare in Yosemite (2024) yosemiteshakes.ucmerced.edu.

Siewers, Alfred K (2014) 'The Green Otherworlds of Early Medieval Literature', in Louise Westling (ed.), *Cambridge Companion to Literature and the Environment*. Cambridge: Cambridge University Press, 17–30.

Shakespeare and Climate Change (2023) Shakespeare Anyone? Podcast www.shakespeareanyone.com/episodes/a-midsummer-nights-dream-climate-change.

Smith, Emma (2019) *This is Shakespeare*. New York: Penguin.

Solnit, Rebecca (2004) *Hope in the Dark: Untold Histories, Wild Possibilities*. 3rd ed. Chicago: Haymarket Press.

   (2023) 'If You Win the Popular Imagination, You Change the Game': Why We Need New Stories on Climate. *The Guardian*. 12 January. www.theguardian.com/news/2023/jan/12/rebecca-solnit-climate-crisis-popular-imagination-why-we-need-new-stories.

Somerset, Alan (1994) '"How chances it they travel?" Provincial Touring, Playing Places, and the King's Men', *Shakespeare Survey* 47: 45–60.

Steingraber, Sandra (1997) *Living Downstream: An Ecologist's Personal Investigation of Cancer and the Environment*. Philadelphia: De Capo Press.

Stopes, Charlotte Carmichael (1918) *Shakespeare's Environment*. London: G Bell and Sons.

Strunk, Kambden K., Leslie Ann Locke, and Georgianna L. Martin. (2017) *Oppression and Resistance in Southern Higher Education and Adult Education: Mississippi and the Dynamics of Equity and Social Justice*. New York: Palgrave Macmillan.

Sullivan, Erin (2022) *Shakespeare and Digital Performance in Practice*. London: Palgrave Macmillan.

Sweeting, Adam and Thomas C. Crochunis (2001) 'Performing the Wild: Rethinking Wilderness and Theatre Spaces', in Karla Armbruster and Kathleen R. Wallace (eds.), *Beyond Nature Writing: Expanding the Boundaries of Ecocriticism*. Charlottesville: University of Virginia Press, 325–340.

Tavares, Elizabeth E., Emily MacLeod and Laurie Johnson (2023) 'Introduction: Properties of Matter and Performance', *Shakespeare* 19(1): 1–7.

*Tender Claws (2019) Video Game. https://tenderclaws.com/theunderpresents.

*The Show Must Go Online (2020) https://robmyles.co.uk/theshowmustgoonline/.

**The Tempest* (2023) Royal Shakespeare Company Website. www.rsc.org.uk/the-tempest/.

*The Theatre Green Book (2024) Renew Culture Ltd. Version 2. https://theatregreenbook.com/wp-content/uploads/2024/03/TGB_v2.pdf.

Thurman, Chris and Sandra Young, eds. (2023) *Global Shakespeare and Social Injustice*. London: Arden Bloomsbury.

Topsell, Edward (1607) *The History of Four-footed Beasts*. London: William Jaggard.

Varma, Rahual (2001) *Bhopal*. Toronto: Playwrights Canada Press.

Waage, Fred (2012) 'Three Studies in Shakespeare Ecocriticism', *South Atlantic Review* 77(1–2): 204–222.

Wald, Christina (2022) 'Shakespeare in *The Wilds*: Experimenting with *The Tempest*', *Adaptation* 15(2): 264–284.

Walmsley, Ben (2013) 'Co-creating Theatre: Authentic Engagement or Inter-Legitimation?' *Cultural Trends* 22(2): 108–118.

Watson, Robert N. (2011) 'The Ecology of the Self in *Midsummer Night's Dream*', in Lynne Bruckner and Dan Brayton (eds.), *Ecocritical Shakespeare*. Aldershot: Ashgate, 33–56.

Weetman, Catherine (2020) *A Circular Economy Handbook*. London: Kogan.

*Werth, Tiffany (2024) 'Eco-Joy in *A Midsummer Yosemite's Dream*'. Oecologies Blog. https://oecologies.com/2024/06/20/eco-joy-in-a-midsummer-yosemites-dream/.

*Widdicombe, Lizzie (2020) 'How Should the Media Talk about Climate Change?' *New Yorker*, 17 October, www.newyorker.com/culture/culture-desk/how-should-the-media-talk-about-climate-change.

Woolery, Laurie (2021) Presentation to the Shakespeare Theatre Association conference. Zoom. 8 January.

Wylleman, Paul, Reints, Anke, and De Knop, Paul (2013) 'A Developmental and Holistic Perspective on Athletic Career Development', in P. Sotiaradou, & V. De Bosscher (eds.), *Managing High Performance Sport*. New York: Routledge, 159–182.

Zalasiewicz, Jan, Waters, Colin N., Williams, Mark, and Summerhays, Colin P. (eds.) (2019) *The Anthropocene as a Geological Time Unit: A Guide to the Scientific Evidence and Current Debate*. Cambridge: Cambridge University Press.

Acknowledgements

We would like to thank Craig Dionne, Erin Sullivan, and Rebecca White for their intellectual and logistical support of this project, and Tiffany Stern, Dan Grimley, and Hedli Nik for hosting Katie in Stratford while this book was drafted. Series editor W. B. Worthen guided our work with enthusiasm, and the two anonymous readers improved the manuscript with helpful suggestions.

We'd also like to thank the cast and crews of the 2023 Royal Shakespeare Company *Tempest* and the 2024 Shakespeare in Yosemite *Midsummer Night's Dream*, and the network of eco-Shakespearean scholars and theatremakers whose work inspires our own. Finally, we are grateful for the loving support of our families: Jeanie and Eireann O'Hare, Larkdale Peggy, and Beverley Freestone; Nancy, Stephen, James, and Isabel Brokaw and Amanda Penabad.

Cambridge Elements ‗

Shakespeare Performance

W. B. Worthen
Barnard College

W. B. Worthen is Alice Brady Pels Professor in the Arts, and Chair of the Theatre Department at Barnard College. He is also co-chair of the Ph.D. Program in Theatre at Columbia University, where he is Professor of English and Comparative Literature.

ADVISORY BOARD

Pascale Aebischer, University of Exeter
Todd Landon Barnes, Ramapo College of New Jersey
Susan Bennett, University of Calgary
Rustom Bharucha, Jawaharlal Nehru University, New Delhi
Gina Bloom, University of California, Davis
Bridget Escolme, Queen Mary University of London
Alan Galey, University of Toronto
Douglas Lanier, University of New Hampshire
Julia Reinhard Lupton, University of California, Irvine
Peter W. Marx, University of Köln
Sonia Massai, King's College London
Alfredo Michel Modenessi, National Autonomous University of Mexico
Robert Shaughnessy, Guildford School of Acting, University of Surrey
Ayanna Thompson, George Washington University
Yong Li-Lan, National University of Singapore

ABOUT THE SERIES

Shakespeare Performance is a dynamic collection in a field that is both always emerging and always evanescent. Responding to the global range of Shakespeare performance today, the series launches provocative, urgent criticism for researchers, graduate students and practitioners. Publishing scholarship with a direct bearing on the contemporary contexts of Shakespeare performance, it considers specific performances, material and social practices, ideological and cultural frameworks, emerging and significant artists and performance histories.

Cambridge Elements$^{\equiv}$

Shakespeare Performance

ELEMENTS IN THE SERIES

Viral Shakespeare: Performance in the Time of Pandemic
Pascale Aebischer

This Distracted Globe: Attending to Distraction in Shakespeare's Theatre
Jennifer J. Edwards

Shakespeare without Print
Paul Menzer

Shakespeare's Visionary Women
Laura Jayne Wright

Early Modern Media Ecology
Peter W. Marx

Sleep No More and the Discourses of Shakespeare Performance
D. J. Hopkins

Staging Disgust: Rape, Shame, and Performance in Shakespeare and Middleton
Jennifer Panek

Extended Reality Shakespeare
Aneta Mancewicz

Approaching the Interval in the Early Modern Theatre: The Significance of the 'Act-Time'
Mark Hutchings

Shakespeare and Nonhuman Intelligence
Heather Warren-Crow

Shakespeare and the Restoration Repertory
Stephen Watkins

Performing Shakespeare on an Endangered Planet
Katherine Steele Brokaw and Elizabeth Freestone

A full series listing is available at: www.cambridge.org/ESPF

For EU product safety concerns, contact us at Calle de José Abascal, 56–1°, 28003 Madrid, Spain or eugpsr@cambridge.org.

www.ingramcontent.com/pod-product-compliance
Ingram Content Group UK Ltd.
Pitfield, Milton Keynes, MK11 3LW, UK
UKHW021322180426
11947UKWH00017B/1387